The author's confrontation with the
varied ills besetting the Indian has
taken many forms, including the
tyrannical bungling of the Bureau of
Indian Affairs; the so-called "termination policy" of 1953 which reneged
on the government's obligation to
render services provided for by
treaties and which further bankrupt
some tribes; a conniving group of
calloused persons—some Indians
among them—who have exploited the
disadvantaged Indian's plight to their
own financial advantage.

Authentic, revealing, thought-
provoking, and bound to cause
controversy, Robert Burnette's book
is a searingly impassioned call for
decency; it must not go unheeded.

The Tortured Americans also includes
a handsome portfolio of photographs
by Richard Erdoes.

THE
TORTURED
AMERICANS

BY ROBERT BURNETTE
"Good Leader" of the
Rosebud Sioux

PRENTICE-HALL, INC.
ENGLEWOOD CLIFFS, N. J.

Designed by Linda Huber
⚓ ⚓ ⚓ ⚓ ⚓ ⚓ ⚓ ⚓ ⚓ ⚓

The Tortured Americans by Robert Burnette

This book is dedicated, above all, to the principles of justice and equality; to my friends who have assisted so ably in the fight for Indian rights: Doris Duke, Ruth Thompson, Alvin and Betty Josephy, Clifford Samuelson, Graham Holmes, and Richard and Jean Erdoes; to my Indian friends, too numerous to list on this page, who stood by me during the most trying times; and to my mother and father, Grover and Winnie Burnette, Sr., who, despite suffering, showed me the richness of my Indian heritage.

Foreword In the decade just past, the tumultuous 60s, this nation began the most painful self-examination since the Union was torn by the Civil War. That probe of the national corpus is still going on and we, like men who fear that life is ebbing, are seeing the sins of our youth and the mistakes of a lifetime pass before our eyes. One area of extreme sensitivity that our probing has isolated is the state and status of minorities—especially non-white minorities—in America today. Old sores to which we have so long applied the unguents of expediency are ulcerating anew, demanding swift and intensive care. As Robert Burnette reminds us here, the festering malignancies discomfiting the Indian in the United States are centuries old and have received the most scandalous treatment. I say this as a black man who carries his own collection of unhealed scars from my own experiences in America.

Many Americans, long made tranquil by the myth that the Indian was vanishing and that those who persisted in surviving were beneficiaries of the Bureau of Indian Affairs' most benign paternalism, have been jolted by the unsettling reality that the Indian is not disappearing, and that the ministrations of the B.I.A. have not stilled the outrage of the people who first "discovered" this continent. Indeed, the Indian population is fast approaching the one million mark (roughly the same number of Indians in the area of the continental United States as when the European explorers first landed), and though a variety of Government agencies supplement the activities of the Bureau of Indian Affairs the condition of Indians remains a national embarrassment. For it is still a disgraceful fact that approximately two-thirds of the Indian population living on the unyielding lands of the reservations are afflicted by poverty (average income is only half of the so-called poverty level), unemployment (almost

7

half the labor force is out of work) and sub-standard housing (over 90 percent of Indian homes fail to meet the criteria of hygiene, comfort and convenience). Not surprisingly, therefore, the infant mortality rate is an appalling 70 percent higher than the average for the rest of the nation. And this does not by any means exhaust the list of deprivations that the Indian has been subjected to, and is still subject to today.

In *The Tortured Americans*, Robert Burnette has not only portrayed, with remarkable control, the plight of the Indian, but he has also sounded an alarm which must be heard—and answered. I pray America is listening.

Alfred E. Cain
Senior Editor
Tuesday Magazine

Contents

"[*An Indian reservation*] *is a parcel of land set aside for Indians, and surrounded by thieves.*" GENERAL WILLIAM T. SHERMAN

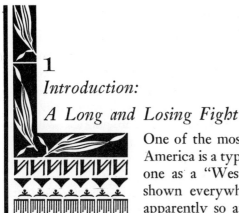

1
Introduction:
A Long and Losing Fight

One of the most characteristic products of America is a type of movie known to everyone as a "Western." Westerns have been shown everywhere in the world, and are apparently so appealing that movie-makers around the globe find it unnecessary to utilize the resources of Hollywood or the American West in the production of such a film, so that they are made thousands of miles from historical sites on Rosebud Creek, in Wounded Knee, or Little Big Horn. In most Westerns, savage Indians outnumber and attack hardy and courageous white men. The redskins invariably lose, many times to the tune of a military bugle signaling the sudden arrival of the United States Cavalry. Indian children, watching these movies, have been observed to cheer when the cavalry approaches at a gallop.

Although battles between white settlers of America and the original Americans were numerous and real, as any schoolboy knows, they bore little resemblance to the Western movies' staging of clashes between whites and Indians, except in one important respect: The Indians always lost the war.

After the end of the nineteenth century, there are no battles whose dates a student can memorize. But a warlike struggle, with the Indian as one of the antagonists and the white man as the other, is still being fiercely waged, and as usual, the Indian is losing. The Indian, though, is at even less of an advantage than he was a century ago. A number of his own, in positions of influence, have gone over to the paleface's side.

Since he laid down his guns, the Indian has no weapons, literally and figuratively. Thus his struggle to retain his heritage and to survive as an individual may seem foolhardy. Faced with corrupt leadership, an indifferent or malicious Bureau of Indian Affairs, and the absence of any legal remedy for wrongs committed against him, surrounded by greedy real estate, cattle, timber, oil, hunting, fishing, and other interests, his capacity to fight effectively is weak indeed. General Sherman's definition of a reservation as a place where Indians live, surrounded by thieves, is tragically true. This book, the record of my experience in Indian politics, with the Bureau of Indian Affairs and with many Indians and whites, both in my own state of South Dakota and around the country, is ample witness to the accuracy of Sherman's observation.

It is painfully ironic to the Indian that at early meetings between Indian and European in the seventeenth century, not only were relations friendly, but Indians actually helped whites to survive and gain a foothold in this country. The usual story is that the Pilgrims, facing starvation in a hostile, unfamiliar land, met an English-speaking Indian, Squanto, who gave them grain and game, and showed them what bounty the new land had to offer and how to cultivate it. The traditional Thanksgiving dinner supposedly commemorates in its choice of dishes the foods the Pilgrim guests in the Indians' country so gratefully accepted from their hosts.

It did not take many years before the white man's religion and his lust for land, which was almost religious in its fervor, clashed with the Indian's quite different notions. Considered to be heathens, the Indians were fair game for bloodthirsty missionaries and clergymen, such as Cotton Mather, who extolled the burning alive of a townful of Indian men, women, and children. The passion to acquire land led to more conflicts, and an obscene and bloody conquest that was to go on for more than three hundred years began.

The Indian, who was not interested in the white man's notion that the salvation of his soul depended exclusively on the white man's religion and its representatives, understood even less the white man's notion of exclusive property. The Indians used the land, apportioned territories in which they hunted, fished, farmed, and lived, but they did not conceive of land as something that an individual owned, sky above and rock below. To the unsophisticated red man, such an idea was an absurdity. The Indians' concept of land has recently gained currency among ecologists and

12

conservationists, who now realize the role the concept of owner-ship has played in the rapid, almost total, pollution of America, above, below, and to all sides. But back at the end of the eighteenth century, the big question facing the newly formed American gov-ernment, after successfully revolting against the mother country, England, was what to do about the Indians. In other words, how could the Indians be civilized, and thus induced to abandon their strange ways and live like other Americans? Henry Knox, Secre-tary of War from 1785 to 1794, suggested that paramount in the process of civilizing the Indian was the development in him of "a love for exclusive property."* But the Indians seemed reluctant to develop this love and become civilized. I experienced, as every In-dian has, the effects of this "love for exclusive property." It is one of the principal themes in this book, which exposes the brazen and cruel exploitation of the Rosebud Sioux.

On July 12, 1775, the Continental Congress—the embryonic government of the United States—formed three departments of Indian Affairs under the geographical headings of North, South, and Middle. The Indian's right to the land on which he stood was clearly recognized by the American government, and commissioners were appointed to "treat with the Indians," ostensibly in order to preserve peace and amicable relations. The first official agency set up by the Confederation to deal with the Indian nations was sub-sumed under the direction of the secretary of war. In 1789, the War Department, freshly created and headed by Henry Knox, was charged with "all matters relative to Indian affairs." The first Bu-reau of Indian Affairs was established by Secretary of War John Calhoun on March 11, 1824. On March 3, 1849, the Bureau of Indian Affairs passed from military to civilian control. In the face of pressure to have the Bureau returned to the Department of War so that a military solution to the Indian problem could be pursued, a commissioner of Indian Affairs in 1868 remarked: "I cannot for the life of me perceive the propriety or the efficacy of employing

* Anthony F. C. Wallace, *The Death and Rebirth of the Seneca* (New York: Alfred A. Knopf, Inc., 1970), p. 160.

13

the military instead of the civil departments, unless it is intended to adopt the Mohammedan motto, and to proclaim to these people, 'Death or the Koran.' "

The early history of the Bureau of Indian Affairs was hardly encouraging. Corruption seemed always to find its way into the Bureau, and in 1865 Secretary of the Interior James Harlan reported that trade with the Indians was being carried on by his staff despite rigorous regulations to the contrary. In 1869, a Board of Indian Commissioners was created to correct irregularities and mismanagement in the purchasing and handling of Indian supplies.

During the first half of the nineteenth century, a great many tribes were forced from their homelands and "relocated" elsewhere. Separating the Indian from the area he considered home was a theme that the paternalistic and all-powerful BIA has played loudly from its inception to the present day. In the eighteenth century, the Iroquois, despite the compliment the whites had paid their political creativity by dubbing them "civilized," had been pushed into Canada and the unhospitable fastnesses of New York and Pennsylvania; the Potawatomies were marched from Indiana to Kansas; the Creeks were moved from Georgia to Oklahoma; the Cherokees, with armed rabble and militia at their backs, followed the infamous "trail of tears" from Georgia and North Carolina to Oklahoma. And so it went. Land for settlers, timber land, oil, dams—all of these interests and dozens of others took precedence over treaties, over families, over tribes and nations who had perhaps enjoyed for tens of thousands of years the land they called home which was now coveted by whites.

Other Indian tribes decided to fight rather than give up their lands. My Sioux forefathers, who had permitted the Lewis and Clark expedition to proceed unhampered across their territories, decided to resist white aggression. They were a proud, religious people who extended respect to all men, regardless of their beliefs or race, and not the savage killers portrayed in white histories and movies. But when they had to fight, they acquired a reputation for being on a par with the finest light cavalry in the world.

On April 29, 1868, the United States Congress and the Sioux nations entered into a treaty which ended the fighting and provided

14

that land be set aside for the Sioux. That reservation was to include the present states of Nebraska, North Dakota, Wyoming, Montana, and South Dakota, with the Sioux to have sole and exclusive use of the territory within those boundaries.

But in 1874 General George A. Custer, leading a reconnaissance party, trespassed upon the Black Hills, which were considered sacred ground by the Sioux, and protected by treaty. Custer suspected that there was gold in the hills, and soon it was discovered that he had been right. A gold rush ensued. The United States government tried to buy the land from the Sioux, who refused to sell. The United States government thereupon condemned the Sioux title to the territory, and the U.S. Army was ordered to collect the bands of Sioux Indians for deportation. The series of battles that ensued culminated in perhaps the most well known battle in the war between whites and Indians—Little Bighorn, at which Custer was decisively defeated by the Sioux and Northern Cheyennes, who were led by Crazy Horse, Sitting Bull, and other chiefs. The end to the Indians' fierce resistance to dispossession from their homes came in 1890 at Wounded Knee, South Dakota, where a party of retreating Sioux was massacred by United States troops. (It is a constant source of irritation to Indians to find in the history books provided them by whites references to "Custer's Massacre," while the atrocity at Wounded Knee is called the "Battle of Wounded Knee," or, according to a sign on Highway 18, "The Wounded Knee Incident." The credibility gap apparently preceded Vietnam by quite a few wars, and this kind of outrageous manipulation of facts has convinced Indians that the white man's words are worthless, whether they are found in a treaty or a history book.)

The white man, superior to the Indian in numbers of men, guns, and bullets, had at last conquered the Indian in the United States, after approximately three centuries of conflict. The Indians were now helpless, completely at the mercy of the United States government, which meant the Bureau of Indian Affairs.

The official purpose of the BIA is stated in Title 25, United States Code, Section 2: "The commissioner of Indian Affairs shall, under the direction of the Secretary of the Interior, and agreeable to such regulations as the President may prescribe, have management of all Indian affairs and of matters arising out of Indian relations." (This power, granted to the BIA by acts of Congress in 1832 and 1866, remains in full force today.)

The BIA attacked their task of administering the country's Indian affairs with missionary zeal. Indian school children were forbidden to speak their Indian language. BIA policemen could enter an Indian's home without a warrant, for the BIA did not consider the protections of the First and Fourth Amendments to the Constitution to be applicable to Indians. Every reservation Indian in the United States was, in effect, living under a dictatorship.

As I discovered personally, the reservation Indian literally had no rights; he could not own anything on his own account and he had no means of protesting injustice. Every aspect of an Indian's life is subject to the scrutiny and control of the Secretary of the Interior's agency, the BIA. According to federal statute, the secretary is the "guardian" of the Indian. For example, any money deriving from land held by an Indian will be held in trust for that Indian by the BIA. The BIA may or may not give that man its approval if he wishes to spend his money. An Indian cannot sell his land without the approval of the BIA. An Indian may not even cut timber on his own land without the express consent of the Secretary of the Interior in the person of his authorized agent, the BIA official.

The Indians, who could no longer fight on the battlefield, could not fight through the courts either. They dangled helplessly between the pincers of the BIA and a singularly destructive piece of legislation—the Dawes General Allotment Act, passed in 1887. This Act instantly reduced in size the land which had been granted to many Indians by treaty.* Named for its sponsor, Henry Laurens Dawes, the bill assigned 160 acres to each head of a family on a reservation and 40 acres were assigned to each of the family head's minor children. Each unmarried Indian over eighteen years old and each orphan was assigned 80 acres. In 1887 approximately 138 mil-

---

* Not all tribes were affected by this act, especially the members of the Five Civilized Nations—the Cherokee, Creek, Choctaw, Chickasaw, and Seminole tribes who had been induced by the Dawes Commission to accept federal and state laws in lieu of their tribal government.

lion acres of land belonged to the Indian; by 1932, after about forty-five years of the Dawes Act, approximately 90 million acres of the original 138 million had passed to white title.

The rationale behind the BIA's bullying and the land grab sanctioned by the Dawes Act was one that would become a theme as monotonous to the Indian as the ancient water torture for assimilation. The Indian was to be assisted by the BIA in sloughing off his heritage as an Indian, a Sioux, a Cheyenne, a Piute, an Iroquois. Strip the Indian of his culture, the BIA supposed, and you would find a creditable imitation of a white man. By removing the Indian's title to his land, the Dawes Act would remove the temptation to fish and hunt, and thus, it was hoped, make a good dirt farmer out of him. The rationales were different, of course, from the reasons. It does not take much sophistication to find a rationale for acquiring 90 million acres of land, especially when the owner cannot do anything to protect his property, and besides, wasn't even an American citizen.

During the last few years of the nineteenth century and the beginning decades of the twentieth, the policies of the BIA and the American government with respect to the Indian rigidified into tyranny. These policies are aptly described by Felix S. Cohan in the *Handbook of Federal Indian Law:*

> The history of Indian service policies is the story of the rise and decline of a system of paternalism for which it is difficult to find a parallel in American history. The Indian service begins as a diplomatic service handling negotiations between the United States and the Indian nations and tribes, characterized by Chief Justice Marshall as "domestic dependent nations." By a process of jurisdictional aggrandizement on the one hand, and voluntary surrender of tribal powers on the other, the Indian service reached the point where nearly every aspect of Indian life was subject to the almost uncontrolled discretion of Indian service officials.

It wasn't until the 1930s that some measure of relief was forthcoming for the American Indian. Early in the administration of Franklin D. Roosevelt, Congressman Edgar Howard and Senator

17

Burton K. Wheeler, along with Secretary of State Harold Ickes, composed a plan to enable the Indian tribes to set up their own governments—which, however, would be responsible to the BIA. On June 18, 1934, the Howard-Wheeler Act, better known as the Indian Reorganization Act, went into effect. It ended the allotment policy of the Dawes Act, and provided encouragement to tribes to create constitutions, by-laws, and systems of self-government. My tribe, the Rosebud Sioux, constructed its government along these diagrammatic lines:

PRESIDENT or CHAIRMAN

TREASURER   VICE-PRESIDENT   SECRETARY

21 Tribal Councilmen (1 from each organized community)

Law and Order Committee   Executive Committee
Health and Welfare Committee   Enrollment Committee
Education Committee   Land Committee

The plan looked splendid on paper, and had the best of intentions behind it. But, in practice, it was doomed from the beginning. The Indians were given a charade to play. No act of the tribal government, except the taxing of its own people, could be performed without the express approval of the BIA. Far worse than offering the Indian people a system of self-government that was composed merely of shadows, it offered them a system in which the Indians who became leaders, because they lacked real political power, found importance and profit by playing upon the greed, ambition, and desire for influence that existed within and without the reservation. Instead of a tribal government, many tribes discovered to their dismay that they had a tribal gang as their representative.

The saddest part of this cruel fraud was the fact that the reservation Indian had *no* legal remedy—no constitutional recourse to protest whatever injustice or crime he might observe or experience. The Indian, although a citizen of the United States under the provisions of the Synder Act of 1924 (a gesture to those Indians who

18

had served in the Armed Forces during the First World War), was explicitly excluded, as an untaxed Indian living on a reservation, from Article I of the United States Constitution.*

During the 1930s and 1940s the Indians supposedly were being baptized into democracy, at least the federally sponsored brand. But the BIA, in the eyes of the Indian, threw obstacles before every Indian attempt to better his physical lot. From 1935 to 1946 the Rosebud Sioux easily could have bought back much of the land that had been lost through the Dawes Act. South Dakota was still reeling from the Depression, and much of the land which had been grabbed so greedily by white homesteaders when it became available was now abandoned. The BIA diverted the Indian's interest from the long-range benefits of regaining the land, and busied itself creating Public Works Administration and Civilian Conservation Corps Indian Department jobs for Indians. Funds in trust for Indians existed and could have been used for land purchases. Instead the BIA oversaw the purchase of thousands of head of low-grade cattle from white ranchers at prime prices, and issued the cattle to the Indians, who called the program (which was sponsored by the ERA or Emergency Relief Administration) "Eat 'em Right Away." Help for the red man turned out, by that magical twist the Indian has learned to expect, to be help for the white cattle rancher.

While the Indian was being denied the opportunity to improve his land base, and was being supplied, in the name of assistance, with cattle no self-respecting rancher would breed, and while many hungry Sioux were searching out jobs, what land they did own (over a million acres) was being grazed by several white cattlemen.

---

* As usual, the United States found a way to make untaxed and taxed equivalent terms. Many of the Indian servicemen in the First World War returned to find their lands confiscated by the state. In the Indian's absence, the government, in order to buttress its "assimilation" policy, had issued "forced patent-in-fee" titles to Indian land. This made the land on which these titles were issued taxable by state and county authorities, and removed the land from the trusteeship, as provided by treaty, of the federal government. When the taxes, of which the Indian soldiers were ignorant, went unpaid, the local authorities "assimilated" Indian land.

These whites paid, not the owners of the land, but some tribal official for this right. In 1936 an inspector from the BIA office in Washington arrived in South Dakota and put a stop to the illegal use of Sioux land. Embarrassed, the BIA fixed leasing policies and placed a minimum price of sixteen cents per acre on grazing land. After congratulating themselves on their fairness to their Indian charges, they promptly forgot about the price. Ten years later, in 1946, the minimum price was raised.

Then, in 1953, the Eisenhower administration introduced the "termination policy" (House Concurrent Resolution 108). This policy was to be the solution to the Indian problem; it was to ensure the Indian's assimilation into white America. Under the provisions of the Termination Bill all United States services to Indian tribes were to be terminated as speedily as possible—including federal trusteeship of Indian lands as promised by treaty. The tribes agreeing to termination would be given money—so much per capita—as an exchange for relieving the government of its obligations. Instant assimilation was the goal of this act. The reservations would be disbanded, services provided by treaty curtailed, and the Indian tribes would find themselves under the jurisdiction of state authorities in civil and criminal matters.

Several tribes acquiesced to the forces supporting termination. Immediately their reservations were full of unscrupulous businessmen—land buyers, car dealers, card sharks—every kind of con man and opportunist one might expect to be drawn to a situation where an uneducated, unbusinesslike group of people were suddenly to have money to spend and land to sell. Stories filtered out of reservations about drunken Indians carrying thousands of dollars in cash around in paper bags. The thieves descended.

Several of the tribes who allowed themselves to be terminated had been well off, even wealthy, before the implementation of this policy. In a typical case, that of the Menominees of Wisconsin, termination brought economic ruin, not because the tribe was quickly infested by thieves, but simply because the tribe attempted to do what the United States government wanted them to do. Alvin M. Josephy, Jr. describes the Menominee disaster in his book, *The Indian Heritage of America:*

20

Almost overnight, many millions of dollars of tribal assets disappeared in the rush to transform the Menominee reservation into a self-supporting county. The need to finance the usual hospital, police and other services of a county and pay taxes imperiled the tribe's sawmill and forest holdings, alienated tribal lands, threatened many Indians with the loss of their homes and life savings, and saddled Wisconsin with a huge welfare problem which it could not underwrite and which had to be met by desperate appeals for help from the same federal government that had thought it had washed its hands of the Menominees.*

Not all the Indian tribes were as short-sighted as the Menominees. Many began to fight against termination—and therefore against those interests which stood to benefit from the results of termination: the oil industry, the timber industry, the cattle industry, the fishing and hunting industry, the real estate industry, to name a few. Although weak and without an effective organization to voice their interests, many tribes fought for their lives as Indians.

The Indians' cause gained an accidental benefit when Albert Grorud, who was on the staff of the Senate Subcommittee on Indian Affairs, came under investigation by a federal grand jury for an alleged $500,000 shakedown attempt on a former Washington attorney, Ernest Wilkinson. Drew Pearson's column, "The Washington Merry-Go-Round," exposed the facts concerning Grorud's alleged activities, and the man was quietly removed from the committee and replaced. The momentum of the termination program had been interrupted and was never regained.

The Indians did have one organization that tried to deter the progress of the termination program, and in general to serve as the lobbying arm for the Indian tribes. The National Congress of American Indians, formed in 1944, undertook in later years to rally the various tribes to united resistance against termination. Although hampered by lack of funds, the NCAI represented the Indians as best it could.

* Alvin M. Josephy, Jr., *The Indian Heritage of America* (New York: Alfred A. Knopf, Inc., 1968), p. 354.

As I grew up on the Rosebud reservation in South Dakota, and entered tribal politics in 1951, I became aware that not very much had changed for the Indian in several centuries. He no longer had to die on the battlefield protecting his family and home; now he wasted away from tuberculosis, drifted demoralized into alcoholism, grubbed what bits and pieces of mean subsistence he could, lived and died impoverished, powerless, ignorant. It was appalling to me to realize how cruelly the promises made to the Indian had been betrayed. Funding a hapless and antagonistic staff of whites to deal with Indians, and pouring money into the pockets of corrupt tribal leaders was undoubtedly cheaper than the estimated one million dollars per dead Indian that was the cost of the late nineteenth-century drive to exterminate the red man.

More than one hundred years have passed since my Sioux forefathers signed a treaty in 1868 with the United States government. The United States government pledged in that treaty to protect the Sioux, to educate them, to provide necessary services, and to keep the lands described in the agreement for the sole and exclusive use of the Sioux. These hollow promises resound today. Congress appropriates money annually in the name of the Indian people. The funds seep on down through the employees of the BIA, disappearing into salaries, autos, office machinery, equipment of all kinds; aside from a road or a welfare payment, the Indian does not see a penny of the dollar he's told has been appropriated for him.

As I write, the conditions on reservations in general and on the Rosebud reservation in particular are the following.

The national unemployment rate among Indians since 1945 has always exceeded 50 percent—in contrast with the national unemployment rate of the United States, which has never exceeded 7 percent.

Until 1961 Indians were excluded from plans for public housing projects. They lived, as many still do, in tarpaper shacks, rickety log houses, ragged tents, abandoned automobile bodies, and hillside caves. When public housing did become available to the Indians, the inevitable corruption that attaches itself like a leech to such projects, made a mockery of the program's intentions. Contractors made extraordinary profits building the houses, construction jobs were used as political payoffs, the tribal leaders and their cohorts soon occupied the best of the houses, and the leftovers, usually defectively constructed buildings, were offered to the people for whom the housing had been intended. As usual, the people last and least.

Health has been and is probably the greatest problem among the Indians. President Lyndon B. Johnson said a few years ago that "the health level of the American Indian is the lowest of any major population group in the United States." Indians have the highest infant mortality rate in the nation—on the average some 30 percent higher than the national rate, and on some reservations the rate of deaths is 100 to every 1,000 births, almost two times the mortality rate in the worst black ghettoes and quadruple that of white babies. The Indian on a reservation has a life expectancy of 43.5 years. The national expectancy is 63.3 years. In South Dakota almost 60 percent more Indians than white die of tuberculosis. Gastritis, enteritis, and other forms of diarrhea cause deaths on reservations in alarmingly high percentages. Otitis media (a middle ear infection that leads to deafness) is common among the Rosebud Sioux, although it was eliminated in other parts of the United States thirty years ago. Hunger and malnutrition afflict large segments of the Indian population. Kwashiorkor, a disease due to severe lack of protein, and marasmus, a wasting disease caused by calorie and protein deficiency, are common on reservations. The present-day health picture of the Indian is so grim one can hardly believe that it exists in the United States, with its vaunted medical technology. To the educated mind, the facts seem to fit some pestilential medieval town, not America of the 1970s. Other health problems include the obvious effects of poverty and demoralization: alcoholism and its attendant diseases, suicide, and drug abuse. Behind these disproportionate disease rates loom conspicuously unhealthy living conditions.

The bureaucratically administered medical care program is an obvious failure. Freshly graduated doctors, who have chosen to serve two years in the Indian Health Service (part of the Public Health Service) rather than in the Armed Forces, provide medical attention on the reservations. In compliance with the rules promulgated by the Secretary of Health, Education, and Welfare, the doctors must constantly make up charts of patients, fill out forms, issue reports, maintain personnel folders, and play internal agency politics. Not much time is left for doctoring. I personally pleaded with the officials in Washington to relieve the Public Health Service doctors of the cumbersome administrative burden by placing a Hospital Administrator at each reservation, thus freeing the doctors for medical duties. The proposal was ignored.

Education is and has been a farce. The overriding purpose of education in years past was to separate the Indian child from his home and his heritage. Children went to schools far from their homes, where they were constantly beaten and threatened into "assimilation." Every Indian child knows, as I did when in school, that "white was right," and generations of Indian children underwent the brutal military training that aimed to destroy the tiniest fragment of pride in one's identity as an Indian. Reform of the educational system in the 1930s meant shifting all Indian boarding school students into programs that were composed half of vocational and half of academic subjects. This hodge-podge assured, as the previous system had, that no Indian student would meet any college entrance requirements. In 1969 the University of South Dakota's Report on "Indian Poverty in South Dakota" stated: "By any standards which can be used, Indian education in South Dakota is a failure." The average Indian over twenty-five years of age has completed 8.4 years in school, more than two years under the national average. A mere 20 percent of South Dakota's Indians are high school graduates—compared to 50 percent of the nation's whites.

The implications are clear to anyone who has undergone the educational experience on a reservation: Indian students, while they recognize the value of education, must, if they have any dignity or pride, resist the kind of training they are subjected to. In addition, it is more likely than not that an Indian child will be ill, poor, hungry, or working, when he is able to, to help his family subsist. Added to these handicaps is the awareness that the goal of the school system fostered by the BIA is not education but acculturation. Never have I known one teacher in an Indian school or one

24

BIA employee who troubled himself to learn the Sioux language or to acquaint himself with the cultural background of his students. Finally, to emphasize the already sad picture of education, the government's failure is dramatized by the fact that the BIA expends $350 per capita to educate Indians, compared to South Dakota's expenditure of $161 per capita and the national average of $149 per capita.

Average Indian income is drastically below the so-called poverty level.* The figure as I write is less than $1,600 per year income. The War Against Poverty and the Office of Economic Opportunity programs have provided illusory assistance. Many families have been fed one month only to discover the next that nothing is forthcoming.

Why has so little material progress been made on Indian reservations? Just how do tribal leaders exploit and the Bureau of Indian Affairs stifle the Indian people? Why can't something be done about it? I asked these questions and lived the answers. This book is witness to two decades in the lives of ten thousand Rosebud Sioux Indians—and representative of the experience of reservations around the country. It documents the fight of a few against the forces of an evil status quo. It is an answer to the ignorant white man who asks me, "How big a check does the government give you every month?" It is an answer to the Indian politico and the BIA official who ask me not to make trouble, reminding me that I, too, could be a smart Indian, a rich Indian, a corrupt Indian. It is a record that I hope will work a change—on my reservation and on others.

---

* A family of four with income of less than $3,600 a year is, by federal standards, a poor family.

2

Initiation

Into Indian Politics

In 1953, at the age of twenty-seven, I entered tribal politics. I ran for and was elected to the Tribal Council, representing the Swift Bear community at the northernmost end of our reservation. I was young and recently out of military service, politically inexperienced but savvy enough to have been surprised by my election. Those in power—both on the council and in higher positions—did not want fresh faces, particularly if they belonged to political independents, in the tribal government. Despite four "certified" candidates, I won by five votes.

Two previous experiences helped to shape my political awareness and aims. These experiences were not unusual; the first was one I shared with other Indians; the second I shared with millions of Americans of all races.

The first experience began when I was five, and as a result of it I learned to fear and hate authority, especially that of the white man, and to use my wits to stave off humiliation and to preserve my sense of dignity. As was the usual procedure then, I was placed in the Rosebud Boarding School in Mission, South Dakota. The school was organized along military lines; dress was a military uniform with a stiff high collar. Severe punishments for trivial infractions were routine, and I came to fear not only the white men but the Indians in their employ. If a child entered the building with wet feet (no one had overshoes) or was late for roll call, his hands would be lashed with a brass-studded two-foot long leather strap. The older boys were given authority over the younger, and of course they savagely beat the children with their belts whenever an excuse could be found.

I learned that for my own protection I had better know how to fight. Fist fights among the boys were everyday occurrences, actively encouraged by the older boys. The school, a benefit of our treaty with the United States government, was less a place of learning than a penal institution designed to break what pride or ambition an Indian child might have. I studied, not to learn, but how to outwit my white teachers. Each day in the school added to my hate for the abuses of authority.

In 1935 my father took a job with the Road Department of the Bureau of Indian Affairs, and we moved our three ragged canvas tents to the Rosebud Agency. I transferred to the Rosebud Day School, which did not inflict the cruel discipline of the boarding schools on its students. Here, at least, I found some incentive to study.

In November 1943 I joined the Marine Corps. At this time I hated whites from the bottom of my heart. The Marine Corps training was easy—I had been through it since the age of five. But this second experience canceled out much of the deep vengeful anger I felt toward whites. Esprit de corps, a war to fight, whatever it was, overshadowed my hate, and I soon become fast friends with young white men from all over the country, north and south, east and west. We endured hardships together and enjoyed ourselves together, and by the war's end I had learned that each man must be judged as an individual.

My early years in boarding school taught me the realities of power, so that I brought to my political career a nose for the odor of corruption and the abuses of authority. If I had been naive, I would have been swallowed up by the backslapping, bribe-giving politicians who passed for leaders; if I had been an idealist without tolerance for reality, my career would have been brief and ineffectual. My Marine Corps experience tempered me, and I knew that there were good men of every race who could be rallied to correct a wrong. Automatic hate or unreasonable hostility would have hobbled my political activity. When I was elected to the Council in 1953, it was absolutely necessary that I be able to see clearly what was going on and to make my plans intelligently.

The eighteen months from early 1953 to mid-1954 that I spent as a councilman were a cram course in the ills that afflict the Indian. It was a complete political education, from the inside, for a young

and inexperienced Indian politician. I saw and grappled with corruption and incompetence in our tribal government; I felt the in-
timidating force of the BIA, and witnessed that Bureau's callous
disregard of the Indian's welfare; I came to know our white neigh-
bors—cattlemen, farmers, politicians, lawyers—and what interests
the Indian held for them; I even became acquainted with Washington, D.C., the seat of power for the American nation, the home
office of the Indian's guardian, the Secretary of the Interior, and
the source of the greatest threats to the Indian tribes.

Our tribal leaders fulfilled every dreary expectation I had. The
president of the tribe, Alfred Left Hand Bull, did nothing each
day but sit at his desk, feet on top, smoking cigars. The tribal
secretary, Antoine Roubideaux, sat before a deteriorated typewriter,
on which he would occasionally type with two fingers. Roubideaux
had enough relatives on the council to be continually reelected
despite the well known and easily observable fact that whenever
he was sent on a tribal mission, he would find the task an excuse
to get drunk. His reputation for public drunkenness at important
meetings was an embarrassment to the tribe.

That spring I was asked to go to Washington with Abraham Bordeaux, Alfred Left Hand Bull, and Antoine Roubideaux, to present
a new program for our reservation to the federal officials. The trip
was a fiasco; we hardly saw Left Hand Bull and Roubideaux, who
spent most of their time drinking, and then had me call the tribal
treasurer to request an additional eighty dollars for expenses. Bordeaux and I tried to get tribal business taken care of, but Left Hand
Bull and Roubideaux managed to interfere with that by barging
drunkenly into a conference at which tribal monies were being
discussed. Left Hand Bull shouted and Roubideaux mumbled. Those
attending the conference just got up and left the room. Bordeaux
and I agreed to make a detailed report on the trip to the tribe
when we returned. That was my initiation as a tribal delegate to
Washington.

The leaders began to realize that I was a potential troublemaker.
I had met resistance from the start; in my first sixteen months as
councilman, the Council rejected every suggestion I offered. I knew
the corrupt officers were thinking of ways to rid themselves of me.

29

In June 1953 I found myself allied with Left Hand Bull on the issue of a pending piece of legislation entitled "Public Law 280." This bill, which would grant the states civil and criminal jurisdiction over the Indian tribes, was so threatening to the Indian that the most unlikely people joined together to fight its passage. We were not surprised that the bill was proposed. "Termination" had been a BIA and federal theme for some time, and the current Senate Subcommittee's Advisor on Indian Affairs, Albert Grorud, a man who seemed dedicated to the destruction of the Indian's integrity, strongly supported the bill under consideration.*

Public Law 280 proposed to place Indian tribes under the jurisdiction of state court systems. It did not matter that Indians were excluded from jury duty by the states. It did not matter that the proposed law conflicted directly with Article XXII of the State of South Dakota's constitution, which declares: "We the People of South Dakota forever disclaim jurisdiction over Indians, so long as there is Indian trust land."

Section Six of the act would give the states criminal jurisdiction over Indians on the reservation, where before BIA-authorized policemen enforced reservation rules. What this meant, in actuality, was that the surrounding white communities, who had never shown the slightest bit of love for the Indian but who did harbor a strong attraction for Indian land, could arrest and imprison Indians on an arbitrary and wholesale basis. The Indian had no legal protection except through the BIA and the United States Attorney, both of which represented white authority. The Indian had been in trouble enough surrounded by white sharpshooters; now it was proposed that he have his hands and feet tied and be set under a spotlight with a bull's-eye painted on his side.

Section Seven of the act would give civil jurisdiction over Indian tribes to the states. Indians would become suable in the state court systems. It did not take much imagination to see what the effects of this section would be. Every double-dealing car salesman, credit operator, loan shark and land shark would be wheeling and dealing at the expense of the Indian, and would be backed by a court

* Grorud was later retired from the Senate Subcommittee, after being exposed in an effort to shake down an attorney for the Utes of Utah.

system which worked on principles and concepts totally foreign to the Indian.

The council opposed passage of the bill, and once again Left Hand Bull and I were chosen to travel to Washington to protest the bill. We drove to the capital, arriving on July 8, 1953. We walked to the hearing room, where we were told there would be no time for our testimony because the witness list was full. We prepared a written statement and submitted it to the clerk. I was furious because I knew the hearings were stacked against those tribal delegations which sought to state their opposition to the bill.

Never in the history of legislation regarding Indians had a bill been enacted by Congress so quickly. On August 15, 1953, President Eisenhower signed the bill, remarking, in view of numerous strong protests by Indians and clergy, that the law was "unchristian-like."

All that the Indian feared soon came to pass. The state penitentiary at Sioux Falls was bursting with young Indians who were serving heavy sentences for crimes that, had they been committed by white men, would have carried the penalty of restitution or probation. Sentences of two to three years in jail for passing bad checks in small amounts—fifteen dollars, for example—were common. The proportion of Indians to whites in South Dakota's prisons quickly swelled to one-third, most of whom had been convicted of minor crimes, and often had been deprived of the constitutional rights that applied to whites.

At this time the BIA was pursuing congressional orders to "terminate" federal services to the Indian tribes. Indians were now subject to the jurisdiction of the state, but the Department of the Interior and the Department of Justice refused to prosecute felonies committed on reservation land. Crimes ranging from cutting fence to rape were ignored by the United States' Attorney's office and complaints were referred to the tribal court system. The Indian thus found himself liable to state prosecution for whatever crimes he committed, but without the same protections for his person or property.

The Indian tribes are supposedly protected by over 389 treaties, 5,000 federal statutes, 2,000 federal court rulings, and more than

2,600 rules and regulations, having the force of law, as well as over 500 opinions issued by the attorney general of the United States. But we were now subject to the authority of hostile local police forces and courts. Nowhere in America is police power, the judgeship, and legal counsel more corrupt, more abused, and more politically influenced than in "Indian country." I have seen it day in and day out, and have known my and others' protests to the attorney general's Justice Department to go unheeded. The effects of the failure of the federal government to make good its legal obligations, and the constant betrayals and deceits, have been devastating to the morale of the Indian.

In my freshman year as a councilman, I had innumerable opportunities to observe—and to resist—the conscious or unconscious disregard of the Bureau of Indian Affairs for the people they were paid to protect. (The appalling situation at the BIA, from top to bottom, with the definite exception of a few good, dedicated people, had not changed at this writing, in 1970.)

While we were trying to cope with the effects of Public Law 280, the BIA was managing to make our lives difficult in big ways and small. For example, about the time of the passage of "280," the BIA, having been ordered to help "termination" along, blundered into a way to put an economic squeeze on the Rosebud Sioux. We had set up and staffed an office which oversaw arrangements of leases of Indian trust lands, a matter very much in the tribe's interest. The BIA appropriated the office and the equipment, saying that such supervision was the BIA's direct responsibility, since no leasing action could be taken without its authorization. The BIA moved its staff into our equipped office, but said not a word about the $49,000 the Rosebud Sioux had already invested in what the BIA now insisted was a federal responsibility.

While our leasing office and our investment in it were disappearing into the hands of the BIA, the BIA was also pressing for the liquidation of loans made to tribal members through the Tribal Credit Corporation. This agency had been funded by money borrowed from federally appropriated funds, and had been intended as help to Indians who wished to start or maintain small businesses, farms, and cattle operations. Now the BIA-controlled Tribal Council Credit Committee was calling back loans, regardless of the stipulations agreed upon by the borrower and the Credit Corporation. As usual, the whole business was performed in a high-handed manner. For example, the Arthur Medicine family, like many others, had their cattle taken from their land without due process of law. The cattle were sold for $14,000 and the $6,480 loan that Arthur Medicine had borrowed was repaid. The remainder of the money simply disappeared. Arthur Medicine had no way of recovering his money or punishing the guilty parties. Many other loans were forcibly liquidated. The intent behind the policy of liquidating tribal loans was the Eisenhower Administration's desire to "terminate" Indian tribes as speedily as possible. This policy was soon instituted on the reservation level.

Here then was the most powerful government in the world, knowing that Indians were wholly without legal remedies, cold-bloodedly wiping out Indian operators who were trying to make a living for their families.

During this period the local agricultural politicians were in full command of the congressional delegations from the states where Indian reservations were situated. It is very interesting to note that in August 1953, when the termination move was made through House Concurrent Resolution 108, not one single congressman or senator made an effort to defend the Indians' position in the final disposition of this vicious legislation.

By the summer of the following year, 1954, the Credit Committee had nearly succeeded in recalling all the money it had loaned out. The tribal leadership had shamefully neglected their duty to protect the members of the tribe. On top of this, in 1953 the Council was served with a notice that the BIA had halted all operations of the Tribal Credit Corporation because this agency was delinquent in repayment of thousands of dollars and over three thousand head of cattle loaned to the Corporation under the tribe's "Repayment Cattle Program." In this program, a client could borrow twenty to thirty yearling heifers, and within five years was required to repay eleven head for every ten that he borrowed.

Now the cattle loan system was defaulted, the opportunity to borrow money was curtailed, and moreover, considerable money

33

and cattle had not been accounted for. The situation was chaotic, and the Indian people felt that the government was summarily abandoning them without a thought to their future. Anxiety, fear, anger, all these emotions were visible among the people on the reservation. It seemed that the disaster of "termination" was upon us. I shared my constituents' feelings, for I too had been a liquidated loan client, and the action had completely disregarded the contract I had signed with the tribe, a contract which had been approved by the BIA. I felt, as the others did, that I had the right to repay the loan in accordance with the stipulations of my contract.

At the end of 1953 the BIA tried to force another scheme on our reservation that amounted to a scalping of the defenseless red man. The BIA wanted the tribe to accept a sliding scale price system that would apply to the leasing of grazing land. The lease price, the BIA proposed, should be keyed to the current market price of beef. If a white rancher needing grazing land contracted with an Indian for one hundred acres at a dollar an acre, and then the following year the price of beef declined by half, that rancher would have to pay the Indian only fifty cents per acre for the grazing privileges. The younger councilmen—some of whom had just been elected in December 1953—fought such a proposal furiously, and when a vote was taken, eight councilmen voted against the provision and eight for it. President Left Hand Bull announced that he would vote to break the tie. Later he said that he voted against the BIA scheme, and we thought the measure had been defeated. The anti-BIA faction of the council adjourned, pleased with their victory.

The next day the BIA superintendent, Will J. Pitner, called Left Hand Bull to his office. When Left Hand Bull returned to the tribal office, he changed his vote to favor the BIA proposal on grazing prices. When this became known, the tribe and the councilmen angrily called for Left Hand Bull's removal. But the council was no longer in session, and under the regulations we could not take any action until the council reconvened, which would not be for another three months.

During that three months I had time to reflect on the previous year, and on the election which had taken place just before the grazing price issue. I had run for the presidency (I was allowed by the constitution to occupy both the council seat and the chair, if I won both elections) but I lost in a close contest—through manipulation of votes, I thought—to Left Hand Bull. But the tribe was tired of the incompetence and corruption of their leaders; Roubideaux had been removed from office, and several good young men —Abraham Bordeaux, Vincent Cordry, Adam Bordeaux, and James Quigley—had been elected to the council. These councilmen contributed a "new look" to our government. I felt that the people were responding to honest leadership that would stand up to the forces of a corrupt tribal government and a dictatorial BIA. The tribespeople had been so firmly under the thumb of their "leaders" and "guardians" that it was hard for them to imagine any degree of autonomy over their own lives and over the affairs of the tribe.

I understood their fears; the BIA brought economic pressure upon me during the three-month intercession of the council. It hoped to break me financially, and thus eliminate a troublemaker. The BIA wished to lease to a white man tribal lands that my father, my brother, and I had leased. We defied the tribe and the BIA by refusing to surrender the lands which we were legally leasing. A loan that I had taken out, $3,300 of which I planned to invest in cattle, had been forcibly reclaimed. Finally the BIA had our lease price raised to one dollar and fifty-three cents per acre, while the going rate throughout the rest of the reservation was thirty-two cents per acre. But the combined forces of the BIA and the corrupt officials failed to break me—financially or psychologically.

During the spring of 1954 several issues came to a head. In April the operation of the Tribal Land Enterprise was scrutinized at the quarterly council meeting. The TLE, which had been begun in 1943 with handsome goals, was empowered to buy and sell land for the tribe, using Tribal Land Enterprise Certificates of Interest as a means of exchange. The certificates worked in much the same manner as common stock, and the TLE would thus make it possible for individual Indians to exchange scattered small land holdings, which they had inherited, for consolidated tracts, which could

35

provide a living for their families. In this way, too, the tribe could buy land from individual Indians who otherwise might have sold their land to whites, thus reducing the Indian land base. The TLE was a fine idea: land to be sold could be acquired by the tribe, and individuals interested in obtaining land could negotiate with the tribe.

But there was too much potential for corruption in TLE. The organization had been buying land from individual Rosebud Indians for eight years, and the certificates of interest which it had issued to the sellers were now worth far less than the fair value of the land purchased; in fact, they were practically worthless. The certificates should have increased, not decreased, in value, as land prices rose. White land buyers and Indians using white money were buying up Indian land for practically nothing, as a result of the TLE's and the BIA's failure.

The TLE's failure stemmed from the fact that the seven-man Board of Directors, which included the president and treasurer of the tribe, had neglected to carry out their legal responsibilities when transacting land business with individual members of the tribe. For example, instead of comparing land prices for Indian lands with prices in sales between white ranchers, they allowed the BIA to appraise the Indian lands at the rate of three dollars per acre on grazing lands and five dollars per acre for farm lands. In sales between non-Indians, prices averaged over thirty dollars per acre.

The Board of Directors approved hundreds of land transactions involving more than 160 acres, for which the Indian received as little as seventy-five dollars. Previously arranged by white farmers and ranchers, these were deals in which the Indian was doing nothing more than giving title to his land to the tribe, in exchange for pocket money that amounted to little more than a payoff made by the person who ultimately got the land.

One Indian, Don Whipple, actually leased 160 acres to a white rancher for $750 for five years, then went to the TLE office where he paid the Indian owner $480 for his land, making a profit of $270 without ever owning the land. The TLE Board of Directors approved of the transaction, and the poor uneducated Indian lost land worth approximately $5,600 at that time. This was common

36

in those days, when under-the-table money was exchanging hands at a very fast rate within the TLE and BIA.

Further, the TLE board were fully aware of the fact that certificates of interests were being traded for horses and used cars and sold for less than par value, but they did nothing to protect the Indian's interest.

While all this illegal land dealing was taking place the final approving agency acting for the Secretary of the Interior, the BIA, was failing to carry out its lawful responsibilities toward protecting Indian trust lands.

To make things worse, the BIA was actually aiding and abetting the corrupt TLE board and the white ranchers by approving land deals for less than a true appraised price, approving TLE certificate sales for less than true value, and executing deeds without proper investigation of details of the sale or exchange.

The BIA made it possible for a white rancher to go to an Indian and make a deal to exchange lands with him, even though the Indian's land was worth twice that of the rancher. This is not to say that some Indians were not taking advantage of the hungry Indian who believed he was going to come into a fairly large sum of money for his land, for many Indians committed the same act as the white ranchers and some became very wealthy during this time. I turned away many Indians who were attempting to sell me certificates for ten cents on the dollar, for I hoped that some day someone would expose these fraudulent land transactions.

Knowing that the tribal members were supporting us, I began to pressure our congressional delegation for an investigation into these TLE land transactions. As a result, an attorney of the House Subcommittee on Indian Affairs came to Rosebud to gather evidence on these corrupt practices. Working with George Abbott, counsel for the subcommittee, Francis Cloudman, Paul Cloudman, Abraham Bordeaux, James Quigley, and I gathered over four hundred canceled checks representing payoffs to tribal officials of the TLE.

Many of us were so encouraged by the fact that over seventeen hundred canceled checks were secured from many ranchers, Indian and white, that represented payoffs to the freewheeling TLE board members that we looked forward to a full-scale investigation that would lead to the prosecution of those who were swindling the Indians.

Being new in politics, I believed that the federal government, the congress, the justice department, and the department of the interior were all strictly dedicated to honest application of justice. I was extremely disappointed when nothing was done, except that Chairman Wayne Aspinall of the House Committee on Interior and Insular Affairs impounded the evidence gathered, which was never to be utilized to this day.

At the April 1955 council meeting we passed a resolution abolishing the TLE and closing its offices. This was a strong action, but the tribe appreciated it. As we filed out of the meeting hall, many of the Rosebud men and women came up to Bordeaux, Cordry, Quigley, and me, and shook our hands. We felt a little closer to breaking the shackles that bound our people in poverty and powerlessness.

Immediately after the meeting, the "moccasin telegraph" brought me the news that the tribal president, Left Hand Bull, and the secretary of the council, Leader Charge, had attended a TLE meeting and were induced to oppose the decision of the tribal council. I believed this report, for both the president and the secretary were on the board of directors of the TLE. I guessed that Pitner, the BIA superintendent, was behind this new development. In any case, the TLE office stayed open.

Pitner's interference in tribal affairs and Left Hand Bull's capitulation to BIA intimidation was first on the agenda of the August 1954 council meeting. James Quigley had visited me in July with a petition calling for a special meeting of the council. He told me the people were demanding that we, the council, remove Left Hand Bull from the presidency on the grounds that he had violated his oath of office.

The facts were obvious: Left Hand Bull had been recorded in the minutes of the Tribal Land Enterprise as voting in opposition to the council's decision to abolish the organization. But according to our constitution, he was obliged to support the decisions of the council. This was the second time he had reneged privately on his own public vote and on a council decision. We all remembered his performance after the meeting on the sliding scale price system for grazing leases, and we knew that if we were to make any headway toward control of our own affairs, Left Hand Bull, and with him, the absolute power of the BIA, must go. I signed Quigley's petition.

The meeting was held on August 13, 1954. That day the councilmen gathered slowly, knowing there was going to be hell to pay. At 11 A.M. a quorum had finally gathered, and Left Hand Bull called the meeting to order. James Quigley rose and formally charged the president and secretary with violations of their oaths of office; he then made a motion to remove Left Hand Bull from the chair until the trial was over. Edward Stands, the vice-president, was to act as temporary chairman.

Quigley explained to the president and secretary that they were charged with acting against the orders of the council when they supported the TLE Board of Directors' decision to oppose the council's order to abolish the agency. They were obliged to honor all council decisions, and therefore they had not fulfilled their oaths to protect the tribal constitution and the best interests of the Rosebud Sioux. Quigley told the two men that they would have an opportunity to defend themselves after the councilmen had testified.

Councilman Henry Eagle Bear stood and said that he believed the president and secretary had acted contrary to the best interests of the tribe and should be considered guilty as charged. Abe Bordeaux expressed the same view. I supported the councilmen, and said that the men should be removed from office.

The president and secretary were given the floor. Left Hand Bull chose to treat the proceeding as a joke, and offered sarcastic remarks about me, characterizing me as troublemaker, as his defense. The secretary simply said that he was not guilty, and that he felt he should not be tried with Left Hand Bull in any case.

A secret vote was taken. The result was four votes to retain the officers and seventeen to remove them. Left Hand Bull and Leader Charge immediately left the room, taking their supporters with them. The meeting recessed for the noon hour.

Excitement was everywhere, as news spread of the dramatic, and

39

for us revolutionary insistence upon principle and the tribe's interest. People swarmed around the councilmen, congratulating us for removing Left Hand Bull and Leader Charge. While we were recessed, the vice-president, Stands, called and resigned. In all, three officers resigned or were removed from office.

When the meeting reconvened, the council was to appoint a president pro-tem. Quigley was chosen, and he made a motion to elect a new president. Abe Bordeaux was nominated. To my surprise, Quigley stood and nominated me. The need to have as a leader someone who would tackle the BIA and fight the federal government's termination policy was discussed.

On the first ballot, I was elected president by one vote—nine to eight.

On the way home, I was still bewildered by the rapid turn of events. A year and a half in tribal politics, and I was now president of the tribe at the age of twenty-eight. I immediately began to wonder what I would find when I checked the records of the tribe's income, its land holdings, its personal property, and its credit corporation.

The next day, the Rosebud Fair was held and proved to be disastrous financially. In an effort to make me look foolish, my predecessors, who had arranged the event, withdrew their support, leaving the management of the Fair completely disorganized.

Though this was not the ideal way to begin my term in office, I tried to concentrate on specific goals toward which I, as president, wanted to lead the tribe. As I was thinking, an Indian woman whom I knew slightly came up to me. I was shocked to see her, because then, and only then, did I remember that early in the year, in January, she had approached me and said that Left Hand Bull would fall in eight months because he had broken promises made in an Indian religious ceremony. She had told me that I was going to be the next tribal chairman (president), and that I would be contacted again about my role as a leader of the tribe. Now she was reminding me of our meeting and the prediction, which I had dismissed at the time.

After the woman left, I continued to think back over the months of 1954. I remembered that in June I had had a strange dream, which was repeated three times the same night. In the dream, a tiny man with bluish skin, about a foot tall, appeared and sat on my left arm. He spoke Lakota, our native language, and told me to follow him, as he wanted to show me something. I struggled to throw him from my elbow, but I could not even budge him. My thrashing disturbed my wife and she awakened me. The dream occurred a second time that night, and my wife told me that again I had been struggling in my sleep. The dreams worried me, and I chose not to tell my wife what they were about. I went back to sleep and again had the same dream. My wife was shaking me when I awoke. I then told her about the dream which now had recurred three times and disturbed me so. I was unfamiliar with Lakota religious beliefs, and the dreams seemed senseless to me, so I forgot about them as the days went by.

Toward the end of June, my father and I had driven to Rosebud on council business. As we were talking to a group of men, a man, the skin around his nose and one eye splotched with pink, came up and requested to see me privately. We walked across the road and he spoke to me in Lakota.

"You had a dream," he said.

"Sure," was my reply, "I have dreams all the time."

"No," he said, "I know you had a dream about a little man three times, because we sent him. You now have the power to be a Medicine Man, but we know you are not ready to do this. When you are ready, come to me and I will show you the way. From now on you will be different"—he touched my forehead—"and you will know things. You will have this power as long as you fight for your people honestly."

I had listened to the man politely, impressed by what he said, but I was also quite puzzled. I had told no one about the dream except my wife, who had not related the dream to anyone else. All the way home from Rosebud that day, the Indian's face and the details of the dream kept recurring in my mind. I learned from my father that the man was Frank Picket Pin, a Sioux Medicine Man.

On Monday, August 16, I learned that Left Hand Bull was going to hold a meeting that day at the fair grounds. I took part of the evidence some of the councilmen and I had gathered against Left

41

Hand Bull and drove to the fair grounds. A crowd of people from the Pine Ridge, Lower Brule, Fort Thompson, Sisseton, and Rosebud reservations had come to hear Left Hand Bull and his faction. I took a seat immediately in front of the speaker's platform, and sat through a series of attacks on our administration, culminating with Left Hand Bull's assertion that he and the secretary had been illegally removed from office.

When Left Hand Bull's people seemed to be running out of criticisms of the current administration, I signaled the chairman of the meeting and asked him if I might speak. He agreed and introduced me.

"My people," I told the crowd, "the tribal council voted me in after removing Left Hand Bull and Leader Charge by a seventeen-to-four vote. It is well known that there could have been other charges placed against Left Hand Bull. Francis Cloudman, Paul Cloudman, and I gathered the canceled checks I have here in my hand, which show that several of our tribal officers and employees have been taking money on the side to push land deals through the tribal offices. I cannot say that I am proud of my new office because it is one that has been used in years past to beat poor hungry Indians out of their land.

"If you Rosebud people want leaders who will sell you out like they have done for these small amounts, then you can have that type of leadership, but as long as I am president no federal or tribal employee will be knowingly allowed to accept side money for land deals. We will have an honest tribal government as long as I have the strength to use my office for the good of the people.

"In closing I should like to say to you that so long as the tribe keeps any drunken leaders on the tribal council we shall not have any respect in the offices of the federal government. I promise that all who are serving as public, federal, or tribal servants will do their jobs or they will be replaced quickly. I am not your master, but I am at your service at any time of the day or night as long as I am your president."

The crowd applauded their approval. My first test was over, and I had passed it satisfactorily. We could now get down to serious business.

During the following days I studied the tribal accounts and records. The tribe owned over 300,000 acres of land, which yielded $17,000 of income under the management of the tribal council and $46,000 under the Tribal Land Enterprise. Thus the land was returning an average of twenty-one cents per acre, while less than forty miles away in Nebraska, grazing land was bringing in two dollars an acre.

Each day hundreds of people would come to my office and complain that the TLE certificates they had been given in exchange for their land were practically worthless. Land grabbing was big business and the TLE board of directors was constantly prearranging land exchanges—for a price. In every deal, an Indian landowner lost his property and was left with promises—in the form of pieces of paper that could not be exchanged for their face value. Nearly twenty times a day I was offered a bribe to push a land deal through. The people who approached me thought of bribery as just part of the business, and evidently they expected me to treat it as a normal function of the office I held. I realized more and more each day that the tribal offices had been a mockery of the concept of serving the tribe; under the apparently blind eye of the BIA, the elected officials served no one but themselves (and those who bribed them). I began to attract surprised expressions and whispers, and I guessed that in many minds ran the thought that I was a strange one indeed for not taking bribes.

The young councilmen and I tried diligently to give the people services and to present to the tribe an example of leadership that worked for their welfare. Abraham Bordeaux became my right-hand man, investigating all complaints and recommending action on those that demanded attention. Quigley, Cordry, and I used each other as sounding boards as we began to develop tribal programs. The older councilmen kept me informed of the mood of the people in their communities throughout the reservation. It was, I thought, an auspicious beginning; the tribal council was working as a team, the needs of the people were being examined, programs to meet those needs were being developed, and best of all, our people were seeing—some for the first time—a group of officials who were genuinely interested in their welfare and in leading them to significant goals as a tribe. I hoped that, for once in the history of our people since the white man arrived, authority would mean considerably more than lies, oppression, and exploitation.

One of my first promises to myself upon assuming office was to rid the reservation of the arrogant BIA superintendent, Pitner. I kept up a steady stream of demands to his office that, as I expected, met with continuous disapproval. Memoranda swirled between his office and mine like a blizzard, and slowly, without realizing it, he gave me the evidence necessary to accomplish his removal from Rosebud.

As my plan to oust Pitner developed, Left Hand Bull kept attacking me, calling mass meetings and maneuvering to topple our administration—all with the help of the BIA, which now was under no illusions that my council could be either manipulated or intimidated. I attended every meeting Left Hand Bull held, armed with evidence of graft and corruption against him and his administration. Through the spring of 1955, his faction attracted less and less of the people to their meetings, while we were gaining the confidence of the tribe.

Early in the winter of 1955, the showdown occurred with Will Pitner, the BIA superintendent. Mrs. Elizabeth Chief, the welfare director, demanded that the minimum requirements of the hungry and the poorly clothed during that cold Dakota winter be met by a program of "Winter Relief," in accordance with BIA regulations. Pitner, however, resisted, and then harassed Mrs. Chief. He sought out employees whom he could coerce into signing unfavorable reports about the woman. I stepped in to take Mrs. Chief's side.

The battle ultimately ended in the commissioner's office in Washington. Pitner was successful, and the commissioner asked for Mrs. Chief's resignation. But Senator Francis Case, who had followed her plight sympathetically, intervened and arranged for Mrs. Chief to transfer into the Department of Health, Education, and Welfare.

As a result of Pitner's action, the council met and demanded his removal. I journeyed to Washington in 1955 and made the tribe's official request, supported by the evidence I had been accumulating, including the official minutes of the tribal council which detailed Pitner's actions during his tour of duty at Rosebud. I smelled victory. The commissioner could hardly deny the evidence before him, and he agreed to remove Pitner from his post at Rosebud.

In December 1955 a new political campaign began. I was nominated to run again for councilman from the Swift Bear community, and started campaigning. One night I was invited by the Two Strike community for what I thought was to be a political meeting. But on my arrival in Two Strike I was greeted by Frank Picket Pin. He led me to a house, a long building built of logs. I knew then that I was to participate in a Sioux religious rite.

Frank Picket Pin prepared ceremonial flags which would be placed in the center of the house. There were four cloth flags, one black, one red, one white, and one green; each flag represented a cardinal earthly direction—east, west, south, and north. The flags were planted in cans of earth, each indicating the direction the flags represented. Then Picket Pin tied his animal token to an ash rod, and inserted this into a can of earth directly in the center of the flags. A large bundle of freshly cut sage was strewn inside the area bounded by the flags, and then hundreds of tobacco knots—a pinch of tobacco wrapped in an inch-square bit of cloth and tied to a string—were placed on the ground so as to form a line from each flag to the others, definitively marking off the central area containing the religious objects.

The ceremony began with Frank Picket Pin praying, as he filled his pipe with Indian tobacco that had been made from the inner bark of the red willow brush. Then several men and women began to sing an Indian song that I had never heard before. Suddenly the room went completely dark and the drumming became louder and quicker.

The participants began singing to God, that He might hear them. I sat quietly, not knowing what to expect. Then, to my amazement, I saw a sparkling light in the room. It moved, blinking on and off, up and down, and suddenly struck the floor at my feet, shaking the entire house. The light touched my forehead four times. I did not move or speak. The singing, in high-pitched Lakota, continued. Suddenly both the light and singing ceased.

Frank Picket Pin, the Medicine Man, prayed for the Holy Spirit to come to him with the answer to their prayers. When he had finished his prayer, each person present prayed aloud, asking that I be reelected as their tribal leader. They described the need for a leader to protect the poor and the helpless who had suffered so long. One woman cried as she prayed for help. I felt an intense compassion for these people, who so earnestly were seeking guidance and aid. As the prayers ended, a song was taken up immediately, and the voices seemed to draw the flickering lights into the room again; the lights struck the floor and ceiling violently, as if trying to break out of the room.

When the song ended, Frank Picket Pin spoke. "The Spirit has answered your prayers, Mr. Burnette, and on the night of the election a man will give you something. Take it and put it into your pocket. You are going to win the election and be our president again. Have no fear, for you will win the election as I have said. But remember, you must not do anything to hurt your people, or you will be hurt in some way." The others at the ceremony uttered a cry as he finished speaking to me—a sign, I thought, that they felt I would figure importantly in the answers to their prayers.

The elections were held the next day. As I walked home, I frankly doubted that Picket Pin's prophecy would be fulfilled. I was confident of retaining my councilman's seat but I did not believe that I would be elected president again.

January 26, 1956, my birthday, was election day. All morning and afternoon a battle raged over the constitutional qualifications of the tribal officers. It was not until 8 P.M. that a motion opened the floor to a consideration of presidential nominations. As the nominations were proceeding, a man I did not know came to my table and handed me a soft bundle of cloth. I took it without looking closely at it, and shoved it into my pocket.

There were three nominees for the office of president, I among them. The ballots were counted, and I was elected by a vote of twelve to nine. Although it was close, it was a clear majority that had elected me. Vincent Cordry was elected vice-president, Antoine Roubideaux, secretary, and Cato Valandra, treasurer. If our people had not swept the elections, we yet were in power, and therefore in a position to continue toward the goals we had set. All

46

but one of the councilmen I considered to be just and honest were returned to office.

It was a happy occasion and my wife invited anyone who wished to come to our house to celebrate my birthday and my victory.

At home, as I was settling down to a piece of birthday cake, the man who had approached me before the elections came up and said, "Look at what I gave you, then give it back to me." I took the bundle out of my pocket, and was shocked to find twelve red cloth tobacco knots—the same number of knots as the number of votes I had received. I recalled the recent ceremony with wonderment, and as I returned the knots to the man a chill flashed down my spine.

3
Programs
and Progress

The year 1956 was still young when the tribe and the Bureau of Indian Affairs discovered that the new tribal administration meant business. I immediately pressed for passage of measures that would double the grazing land rental rates, which formerly had been pegged at giveaway prices. The council supported the new rate, and recommended to the BIA that they increase lease rates on behalf of all Indian landowners. We won our increase, and our people were surprised and pleased to find their rental checks doubled within such a short period of time. We were proving that a council dedicated to the needs of the tribe could gain immediate results.

The older, more conservative members of the council found our newly acquired aggressiveness contagious, and they too began proposing that the returns from business done on Indian land be raised to fairer proportions. A resolution was submitted to raise the farmland rental price from one dollar and twenty-five cents to two dollars per acre. It didn't take long for the opposition—local white ranchers and farmers—to form. They, together with the South Dakota congressional delegation, howled that the "young rebels" in the tribe were trying to take over. We were amused by this cry of outrage, protesting that Indians, on their own reservations set up by acts of congress, were trying to "take over" what supposedly they already were entitled to.

But the threat from the local whites, who had political pull, had to be met, and once again I was sent to Washington to defend our position. This time, I decided, I would not patiently and painfully wait in lobbies until the officials had made up their minds that they could meet with an Indian. Instead, I walked into whatever office I wished and demanded to see the BIA official in charge. I can still remember the shock on the white faces when an Indian appeared

49

who had the nerve to treat them as public servants who were being paid with money appropriated for Indians. I succeeded in convincing them that our position on lease rates was fair and long overdue. Moreover, when I returned home, I learned that other tribes throughout the country had taken notice of our action, particularly because it was interpreted as defiance of the hitherto all-powerful BIA. Morale was as important as money, and we on Rosebud had shown that firmness could improve both of those long-standing deficiencies in the Indian's life.

At this time we received assistance from a white person, whose generosity and concern I still cherish. An article appeared in *Look* magazine, exposing the terrible conditions under which the Rosebud Sioux lived. Coincidentally, I went to New York to apply for grants from various foundations in order to supply several of the tribe's most pressing wants. I chose the Doris Duke Foundation from a list of such organizations in the phone directory, and went to the foundation's office, where I talked about the conditions on our reservation for over an hour with Miss Sophie Van Theis. She had read the *Look* piece, and after listening to me, said, "I have a friend who would like to do something for the Rosebud Sioux that would cost about three thousand dollars and that the people could use and see every day."

I answered her immediately. "We could use a ton-and-a-half truck to haul surplus government commodities to the twenty-one communities." Our people were hungry and in need of clothes, and delivery of surplus supplies was taxing tribal funds that otherwise could be used to improve the overall financial situation.

Miss Van Theis asked me to go to my hotel and write up the benefits that such a truck would provide the tribe and come back to the office that afternoon. I did as she asked, and she gave approval of the truck immediately after reading my report. I could hardly believe that something we needed so badly had been given so simply and humanely, without red tape, promises, and the begging that we often found in our dealings with many "concerned" whites. A month later, I picked up a new GMC truck from the factory in Detroit and drove it to Rosebud.

We were to be the beneficiaries of Miss Duke's compassionate interest in the Indian again and again, and certainly some of the inevitable hardness I felt in my heart for white people relented. I realized anew that men, whatever their color, must be judged as individuals.

Later in 1956, when I traveled to San Diego to serve as an adviser for the formation of the California Inter-Tribal Council, I had the opportunity to meet Miss Duke. She was quite gracious, and sincerely cared about the Indian's plight. It seemed to me that if there were white people whose position and wealth enabled them to be of assistance to our cause—and here was proof that there were —our battle would not be as lonely and lacking in resources as I had thought.

Through the spring of 1956 the tribal council continued to move swiftly and strongly. We arranged for the purchase of vegetable seed for the needy on the reservation; the purchase was approved of a used station wagon to serve as an ambulance, for the majority of the people on the reservation had no way of getting to the hospital.

Will Pitner, the BIA superintendent we had ousted, left the reservation. Pitner was replaced by Guy Robertson, whose qualifications for the job included the administration of the Heart Mountain Camp for the internment of Japanese citizens during World War II, under the auspices of the Japanese War Relocation Agency.

Robertson soon revealed his prejudices, and my office was flooded with complaints from tribe members who charged that the new superintendent threatened and harassed them, making generous use of the usual insults of "laziness" and "drunkenness." I remember going into his office one day with Henry Eagle Bear and his family in an effort to obtain approval of a lease agreement. Robertson became angry as we made our proposal and said, "I will not approve advance leases for any damn drunk Indian who will not get out and work." Then and there I made myself a promise that Robertson would be removed. Not very long after that incident, I learned to my amusement that Mrs. Carrie Moran, an Indian lady, had chased Robertson around his desk after he had called her a drunkard, and help had to be summoned for the United States' "guardian" of the Rosebud Sioux.

Robertson's transfer was high on my agenda, but there was a good deal else to do. We instituted an eyeglass program to help hundreds of school children and adults who badly needed, but did not have the money to purchase, glasses. We evolved an "Emergency Short-Term Loan Program" so that the people could obtain money needed to meet the many relatively minor needs and crises that occurred from day to day. These included replacing broken windows, travel expenses to seek out-of-state summer employment, sickness and funeral expenses—all loans that had never before been available to the people on the reservation.

Another priority activity on my agenda was to make some attempt to deal with the problem of our Tribal Land Enterprise operation. When it became apparent that opposition to the council's policies was almost nil, and I felt we had the overwhelming support of the people, I decided it was time to act. A select committee of councilmen, headed by Jimmy Quigley and Abe Bordeaux, had been investigating the entire TLE operation for some time. This committee produced a detailed report on the TLE's corruption, including a note that an audit could not even be completed because of "lost records." Now we needed an emergency situation, in which a tribal member held stock in TLE, to make our move. I knew a family whose teenage daughter had just died. The man needed money for the funeral. He came to me and we both went to the superintendent, Robertson. I explained that the man held TLE shares that could be purchased with the tribe's TLE funds, and that he needed the money to bury his daughter. I asked if we could arrange to have TLE buy his shares for cash. Robertson apparently was caught off guard, for he agreed, provided the transaction was allowable under the TLE bylaws. I quickly signed a petition for the approval of the purchase of the man's TLE shares, and took it to the board of directors. As president of the tribe I was automatically on the board of the TLE, and I was able to gather four of the board members' signatures without too much resistance. I submitted the petition to the chairman of the board, George Kills In Sight, who prepared a voucher necessary to draw a United States Treasury check to the order of the bereaved father. The check was given to the man. Never before in the history of the tribe had a tribal member received cash for certificates issued by TLE.

After this breakthrough, the next step was to have a true value placed on the TLE shares. We knew that the BIA appraisals were about 75 percent short of a fair evaluation of the certificates' worth. The Indians felt they were being robbed by their own guardian appointed by the United States government to protect Indian interests, and who had full responsibility for appraising and approving the sale of Indian trust land. The BIA also controlled the activities of TLE, and had allowed Indians to sell their TLE certificates for 10 to 25 percent of their acknowledged value of one dollar per share.

The tribal council supported my proposal that we fight for full par value on all TLE shares. The BIA, we now knew, would approve the sale of TLE shares for cash. Then they arbitrarily set a price of $1.43 for each TLE share, evidently feeling that such a price, forty-three cents over the original par value per share* in 1943, would reflect the rise in land values since that time, and be recognized as exemplary of the agency's fair treatment of its wards. But we knew very well that the BIA was appraising Indian land at three dollars per acre, and that land owned by white men, both within the bounds of our reservation and adjoining Indian land, was selling for fifteen to thirty dollars per acre. A good many Indians considered the very admission by the BIA that the TLE certificates were grossly undervalued as a victory.

We took another tack in our project to correct the abuses of TLE enterprise. The tribal council was considering a resolution to amend the TLE bylaws, so that the board of directors would no longer have the power to reelect themselves; instead, the board would be elected by the councilmen who represented the tribe, the actual owner of the land. The BIA energetically opposed us and supported the TLE board members. The council retaliated by again voting to abolish the entire organization that in its thirteen years of existence had lost more than 200,000 acres of Indian land.

* The ratio of shares to land was three shares per acre.

The BIA reacted furiously, and although we were not able to close the TLE offices, the tribe began to recognize a transformation in themselves and in their leaders. We were reestablishing the spirit of our forefathers, the old Sioux, who were known for their pride, their courage, and their concern for their fellows.

The spring of 1956 brought me the opportunity I had been awaiting. I had saved Superintendent Robertson's memoranda documenting his arrogant and unwarranted attacks on both individual Indians and the race in general. I had innumerable witnesses to the man's bullying and rudeness. Armed with this evidence, I got Commissioner Glen Emmons to secure Robertson's transfer. Emmons remarked to me as I sat in his office, "Mr. Burnette, you people have gone through two superintendents in eighteen months. Who *can* you get along with?" I suggested Graham Holmes, a man who I knew was fair and understanding. Emmons ordered Holmes transferred to Rosebud.

Ironically, a few days after the transfer of Robertson, who had constantly harangued Indians for drunkenness, nearly two hundred empty whiskey bottles turned up in the basement of his government house. Yet, even upon leaving, Robertson left a memorandum to his successor, characterizing the Rosebud people as lazy drunkards, and describing me as a troublemaker.

In December 1957 nominations were made for tribal elections scheduled for the following month. I was urged to run again for president, and to continue the programs our administration had begun. Early in December I attended a religious ceremony in the Parmelee community, and as Medicine Man Frank Picket Pin had done years before, a full-blooded Sioux named Rudy Runs Above made preparations for the rite which would predict the election's outcome. During the ceremony he came up to me and said, "You are going to win the chair again by a vote of 16 to 5." On January 26, 1958, sixteen councilmen voted to reelect me as their tribal president.

The same people who had done so much during the previous administration to enact reforms on the reservation were reelected with me. We immediately resumed our program, and this time we would not have a prejudiced and unsympathetic superintendent to oppose every proposal that promised the Indian a fair deal.

The council enacted an ordinance amending our tax system, so that the tribal tax rate of two dollars per quarter section of land (160 acres) levied on lessees of Indian land would now be raised to 5 percent of the total lease price paid for each tract of land used for grazing. Farmland was to be taxed at the rate of 20 percent of the price bid to lease the acreage, instead of the antiquated rate of two dollars per 160-acre section. The new tax structure increased tribal income by approximately $80,000.

The tribal government could afford to serve its people as it had never been able to before, and it immediately met one of the reservation's sorest needs: an adequate police force. Previously, one policeman had responsibility for patrolling the entire reservation. We hired a total of twenty-one policemen, one for each of the communities on the reservation.

I presented a resolution to the tribal council that would withhold four large tracts of tribal land from the range unit system. Under the provisions of the Indian Reorganization Act, the Secretary of the Interior promulgated regulations whereby both tribal and individually owned lands were placed in usable-sized blocks of grazing areas that were advertised for sale to the highest bidder. Although there is some question on the legality of such a procedure, deriving from paramount individual constitutional rights, this practice has been in force since 1935.

The individual Indians have generally opposed such a program because it barred them from securing the highest price possible by forcing them to give the BIA a power of attorney and thereby placing them in the position of having to accept the over-all bid. Many times, Indian people have challenged the system, only to find that their money is withheld until they sign the power of attorney. In other words, it was comply or starve.

This system of grazing regulations is grand for ranchers, for it is a made-to-order bargain through which they can secure blocks of land without bothering with the landlords. And what is more, they are protected by a five-year contract with the BIA.

55

In our attack on this system, we advertised these parcels for rent, asking for bids and reserving the right to reject any bid that was not satisfactory. As a result, a contract was negotiated and signed leasing the land to a big firm from Sioux City, Iowa. Thus an additional $60,000 went into the tribe's coffers.

These new—and, from the point of view of many local whites, revolutionary—developments of Indian self-confidence and self-assertion did meet with resistance—not, happily, from the BIA, but from white farmers and ranchers who, of course, were going to have to pay a little more and profit a little less from Indian land. However, the Assistant Secretary of the Interior, Roger Ernst, supported our position on the tax ordinance, stating that tribes could tax anyone doing business on their reservations, and his opinion was upheld by the Federal Courts of the United States. The white ranchers and farmers battled us for eight months before the court ruling was made that gave the Indians a long-awaited taste of victory after their many losing battles with the "calvary."

We did lose some important fights, however. A plan had been proposed to decrease the size of the reservation by ceding the eastern counties of Tripp, Gregory, and Lyman to the United States, provided that land held by each individual Indian in those territories was treated as trust land as long as the individual desired. The tribe would give up all mineral, water, and hunting rights within that territory for $6 million. Our plan was to use the money to buy other land that would provide more advantages to the tribe. Committee hearings on the proposal were held in the state before the bill reached the United States Congress. The local white interests, which did not under any circumstances want Indians accumulating land of their own choice or competing with white buyers for real estate, succeeded in having the area's congressman, E. Y. Berry, refuse to introduce the proposal in Congress.

When I thought back over the years from 1954 to 1958, I realized that the tribe had come a good bit closer to managing their own affairs and creating a community that would not be dominated by the BIA, local white interests, and corrupt Indian leaders. A multimillion dollar school was planned to replace the delapidated (and condemned) Rosebud Boarding School that had been built in

1884; a sound plan was being developed to borrow $500,000 in order to buy land from tribal members who wished to sell, thus keeping the land in the tribe's domain. The tribe's income had been increased considerably; we had a police force, new equipment necessary to the welfare of the tribe, and a sympathetic superintendent. Then, to top everything off, Doris Duke offered to help the tribe purchase cattle, and we added 172 head of two-year-old white-faced Hereford heifers to our assets. She also offered us a gift to be used to better the health of our people. I suggested that a bus would be a valuable gift, to be used to bring all those who wished to go to the hospital for examination or treatment on a regular schedule. In a matter of days we had our bus, which would serve hundreds of sick people each week who before then had no opportunity to seek medical attention unless they were so ill an ambulance had to be called. The "young rebels" who came to power in 1954 had achieved a good deal, I thought. Nineteen-fifty-nine was to bring new challenges, new battles, and I was to learn how fragile an Indian's victory can be.

In February 1959 I once again journeyed to Washington. I was to meet with Roger Ernst and discuss the possibilities of a substantial loan to our tribe. I picked up a copy of the Washington *Post* shortly after arriving in the city, and read, to my surprise, that an amendment to the Johnson-O'Malley Act was being presented in the House of Representatives. Passage of the amendment would mean terror and tragedy to the reservation Indian. The Johnson-O'Malley Act, in appearance beneficent, provided funds for Indian education, a school milk program, and the like. Now, under this benign cover, it was proposed that federal funds be supplied to states for the purpose of maintaining "law and order" on Indian reservations. We had already experienced the injustices perpetrated by Public Law 280 (1953), and now the poisonous potential of this new law was to be released by means of federal funds.

I hurriedly made arrangements to testify before the Interior and Insular Committee's Subcommittee on Indian Affairs. I knew that if this amendment became law, all Indians on reservations would be at the complete mercy of state authorities, whose primary aim would be to divest the Indian of his land and to destroy the tribal system. I imagined Indians in state courts, facing a jury of whites; Indian children taken from their parents and placed in foster homes; Indian children in schools dedicated to the eradication of their heritage; wholesale discrimination against Indians and the Indian way of life. I decided to make my testimony a report of the injustices that had occurred since Public Law 280 had been enacted. I had evidence to support my charges, but I knew that such testimony would arouse anger and outrage that would have lasting reverberations at home. Nevertheless, five years of open and vigorous fighting had brought results, and it would be not only cowardly but unwise to shrink at this time from a direct assault on a legal weapon that whites had fashioned to harass, subjugate, and ultimately devastate the reservation Indian.

When I was called to testify I told the committee that I opposed the proposed legislation. I told them that states which contained Indian reservations were incapable of policing the reservations without prejudice, and that federal funds would be used in the service of discrimination, not justice. I recounted the following specific incidents.

Indians are arrested on a wholesale basis, because officials are paid mileage fees for each arrest on a reservation. On the Rosebud reservation there was a typical case in which three Indians were arrested, and taken, *one at a time*, to the county jail forty-two miles away. A charge of fifteen cents per mile was levied on each of these trips.

Indian women have been attacked sexually while in jail. A fifteen-year-old girl became pregnant after such an attack.

Indian men are brutally beaten and chained while in jail.

Jail sentences for Indians are grossly disproportionate, when compared with similar convictions and sentences for whites.

Indian life is cheap in the eyes of the local authorities. An Indian who murdered another Indian was sentenced to four years in the state penitentiary. A white man, "Nig" Ryan, killed an Indian and was sentenced to a one hundred dollar fine and thirty days in jail. Another white man shot an Indian in the back seven times, killing him, and received two years in the penitentiary, of which he served six months. A white man who stole a saddle was sentenced to five years.

Since reservation Indians are not on the tax rolls, they are excluded from jury duty, and therefore it would be futile for an Indian to expect trial by his peers.

I pointed out that after Public Law 280 went into effect, states hastily acted to assume jurisdiction over reservations without amending their constitutions, which disclaimed jurisdiction over Indians on trust land. I reported the discrimination that existed against Indians in the hiring practices of state highway maintenance crews and construction and government offices. Indian people whose heritage and education did not include an understanding of the white man's legal and social systems,* would be totally unprepared to shift immediately to such systems, and, I said, the passage of the bill at hand would set our people back thirty years and create new and pressing racial problems. I asked that legislation be rejected, and thanked the committee for opportunity to present my views.

Chairman James Haley requested that I furnish the committee with evidence to substantiate my statements. I assured him that documentary evidence supporting each assertion I made would be provided to the committee. Congressman Haley, a Democrat from Florida, commented that he wished that a colleague from South Dakota had been present, as Northerners were always charging the South with discrimination, while they discriminated against the Indian. The committee recessed.

I went to the office of Roger Ernst, the Assistant Secretary of the Interior, to press the tribe's case for a $500,000 loan. A re-

---

* Before the whites conquered the Indians there were no jails, no courts. If an Indian committed a crime against person or property, appropriate restitution was demanded and the criminal suffered social disgrace. Punishment for its own sake was not practiced. The society was strong and respected enough to deter crime and to encourage virtue.

59

volving loan fund program for Indians had been begun in 1934, with a $2 million appropriation. Over the years the fund had grown to $7 million. But it was a well known fact that during the six years previous to 1959 not one application for a loan had been approved. The funds were "frozen" by the Bureau's obsessively rigid insistence on bank procedures which demanded that applicants provide 100 percent collateral, and thus for the Indian the program was entirely unsuccessful. When loans had been made prior to 1953, the national loss was below 1 percent, but the BIA saw this as reason to make the regulations so stringent as to practically deny all loans.

Ernst was sympathetic to our needs and fair about regulations. He welcomed me and we talked about my appearance before the committee. He agreed that it was dishonest, as well as cruel, to hide a bill concerning criminal jurisdiction beneath a bill that provided educational facilities, including a food program that enabled thousands of Indian children to attend school without having to go hungry. He advised me to gather all the evidence I could and report it to the committee.

In this understanding atmosphere, we discussed the loan. We wanted the money to purchase land from individual Indians who wanted to sell, and thus preserve the Indian land base, rather than have it slowly but surely eroded by a steady sale of individual land to whites. We could not afford to lose more land to non-Indians, for we would then be placed at their mercy in our efforts to obtain reasonable lease prices. I explained in detail the purposes and plans for the money.

Ernst said that the Bureau would undoubtedly raise objections to the loan, but if we drafted the application so that all reasonable questions would be satisfactorily answered, he would approve the application.

When I left Ernst's office and prepared to return to South Dakota, I felt confident that we had an excellent chance to have the loan granted, and I also felt that the amendment to the Johnson-O'Malley Act might run into more trouble than the sponsors of the bill figured on.

Back in Rosebud everything seemed to be proceeding as usual. My family of nine was up at 6:30 in the morning, the children went off to school, my wife left at 7:45 for her job at the U.S. Public Health Indian Hospital, and I walked over to the tribal office. A large group of people, as usual, had gathered outside the office. Jesse Good Voice, the interpreter for the Bureau of Indian Affairs Probate Division, always arrived at 8:00 A.M. on the dot. I talked to Mr. and Mrs. Joe Kills The Enemy, who had come from the Upper Cut Meat community seeking payment for land sold to the tribe. Henry Big Crow, a councilman, met with me privately on the presentation of a resolution which would provide vegetable seeds to families who could not afford to buy them. A small delegation of people from the Milk's Camp community invited me to a meeting to report on my trip to Washington. People from the Horse Creek community, the Antelope community, the Swift Bear community, the Bull Creek community, the Two Strike community, the Grass Mountain community, the He Dog community—in fact, from all the reservation's five counties and twenty-one communities—came to ask questions, to present problems, to seek advice. And so the day went.

Each day at the office was painful, for every minute I was forcefully reminded that the majority of my people lived in almost unendurable conditions. Well over 50 percent of the men never have had the opportunity to hold a steady job—and a good job was one that paid five dollars per *day* for fourteen hours of work. Some people came into the office who were literally starving, others had had no food but government surplus for as long as they could remember.

The office was the scene of many heartbreaks. We maintained one of the few telephones on the reservation, and messages frequently came through, reporting deaths, illnesses, and the like, which we had to communicate to the relations. Funerals were arranged through my office, as well as use of the tribal ambulance. Dealing with the problems of sick people, an understaffed, overbureaucratized medical staff, and an inadequate hospital was probably the most heartbreaking job of all. The waiting room of the

61

Public Health hospital was always so jammed that someone requiring only a prescription would have to wait five hours. Because the doctors did not have space or time for proper treatment, people often died immediately after being released from the hospital. Our tribal ambulance was sent out one day to bring eighteen acutely ill babies to the hospital. They were treated and discharged the following day. All died hours afterward.

My first day back permitted no time to begin the business that had accumulated while I was in Washington. The loan would require immediate attention. A staff meeting must be called, and the Tribal Land Enterprise employees put to work gathering data that would justify the loan. The tribal treasurer had to begin preparing an up-to-date financial statement for the same purpose. A map had to be drawn showing every tract of Indian trust land. The entire tribal staff had to be notified that they would be working overtime to produce the report that would be presented to the committee, as it had requested, and to prepare the loan application. I left my office exhausted.

The next day, as I entered my office, the telephone rang. Even before I picked it up I knew there was a battle with the state of South Dakota in the offing. A friend from Pierre, the state capital, was on the other end, and he informed me that the news media were carrying the full story of my testimony in Washington. I did not need to be told that the state legislators were enraged. Vehement denials that discrimination existed in the fair state of South Dakota were being issued instantly. One state senator, my friend reported, had thrown his morning newspaper across the senate floor and viciously cursed all Indians. As I placed the receiver down, I had the feeling that a controversy was about to erupt that would change my life and my career.

The wisest move, I thought, was to show up in the state capital immediately. It would be significant if all the Indians in the state presented a united front, so I called the tribal leaders and asked them to come to Pierre too. Three miles out of my town, White River, a member of the Oglala Sioux and director of the state Office of Indian Education, John Artichoker, Jr., waved me down as he passed. I backed up to meet him, and he told me that he had been on

62

his way to Rosebud to see me. The legislators, he reported, were threatening to kill the Indian scholarship appropriation of $44,000 on account of my testimony. I was very angry to hear this, although this kind of retaliation to the Indians when they refused to go along with white interests was to be expected. I told Artichoker that I was on my way to Pierre with a stack of affidavits and a recent report from the University of South Dakota's Institute on Indian Studies, to see the governor, Ralph Herseth, and prove to him that my testimony had been of facts that could be documented.

I had confidence in the governor's fairness to the Indian. The governors of North Dakota, Montana, Minnesota, and South Dakota once had held a conference with the department of the interior, the subject being the high cost of welfare payments disbursed to Indians in those states. Governor Herseth surprised the other members of the conference by appearing with me, the only Indian to attend the conference. The others attending the meeting obviously felt uncomfortable, as if they could not really speak their minds. Herseth told the others that I was there to advise him on facts related to his own state. Minnesota had a heavy burden of welfare payments to Indians (mainly as a result of termination); its governor and the governors of the other states present had hoped to maneuver to evade responsibility for these payments. But the plan fizzled, and the subject of the conference was filed, not to reappear.

I went to Governor Herseth's office and he received me. We discussed the details of discrimination against Indians in the state. I reported specific cases and gave the names of law officials involved. He acknowledged that his white constituents were pressing him to fight the adverse publicity given to the state, but he did not deny the evidence I presented to him. I told him that the state legislators were preparing to reject bills that would benefit the Indian significantly. He assured me that that would not happen, and indeed, the bill providing an Indian scholarship fund was passed that afternoon. By the time I left Herseth's office, the other Sioux delegates—from the Oglala Sioux, the Flandreau Santee Sioux, the Sisseton Sioux, the Lower Brule Sioux, the Standing Rock Sioux, the Crow Creek Sioux, and the Rosebud Sioux (my tribe) had

63

gathered outside of the governor's office. Only the Cheyenne River Sioux and the Yankton Sioux were absent. I briefed them on the development of the controversy and told them I intended to file documentary evidence supporting my testimony with the congressional committee within the next two weeks. The delegates pledged their support and congratulated me for revealing to the nation the ugly facts of prejudice and discrimination in the state. The tribal representatives offered me evidence of discriminatory occurrences on their reservations.

The next day I had the honor of being attacked on the editorial pages of just about every newspaper in the state. The Sioux Falls *Argus Leader* denied that any discrimination existed in the state. The Rapid City papers were even stronger, accusing me of lying. Even a Sioux Indian, the Aberdeen area director of the Bureau of Indian Affairs, Ben Riefel, issued a strong denial of the existence of racial discrimination in the state. This statement really shocked me, for Riefel had spent a great deal of time in 1952 battling discrimination against Indians along the Nebraska-South Dakota border. He had succeeded in getting many of the "No Indians Allowed" signs removed from public places in that area, and therefore his denunciation of my testimony saddened me. The BIA tends to make Uncle-Tom-a-hawks of us, I fear. I turned to the business at hand: preparing the report that would silence those outraged voices, and perhaps provoke some thought about how to correct injustice, instead of simply denying or ignoring it.

During the days spent gathering and recording evidence other problems arose. The local white ranchers banded together to form the Todd County Tax Payers League. They were going to refuse to pay the taxes that we had lawfully levied on the use of Indian land. Our patience was short, and we retaliated by announcing that all persons belonging to the Tax Payers League would henceforth be denied the privilege of leasing tribal lands. It was, for us Indians, a revolutionary proclamation. It worked. There was too much money to be made from Indian lands, even with a tax, and the League dissolved like snow in May. I had made some lifetime enemies and would have to keep a sharp lookout for remnants of the Todd County League. But I figured if the tribe progressed toward self-sufficiency at the same rate I was making enemies, I might be able to retire from the presidency in a few months.

Finally, I packed my bag and headed for Washington (by now my second home and unbeknownst to me at the time, soon to become my first), report in hand. In Washington, I met with the tribal attorney and we produced a statement for the congressional committee, incorporating state court records, affidavits by injured parties, and a copy of the report on discrimination against Indians compiled by the University's Institute on Indian Studies,* which contained signed letters from several judges of the Circuit Court of South Dakota, blatantly expressing anti-Indian sentiment. (One judge remarked that he would not allow Indians on juries because they were unfit for civic duties.) The statement was delivered to Chairman Haley. He read it, and thanked me for documenting my testimony. The amendment to the Johnson-O'Malley Act was filed and, I hope, forgotten.

The controversy reached new heights in South Dakota when the United States Civil Rights Commission, through its office in South Dakota, announced that it was going to hold hearings in Rosebud on the charges contained in the report. The hearings began at once, and a great many Indians came forth to confirm the truth of the charges. But just when we thought a breakthrough for fair treatment of our people by the local authorities was imminent, the politically appointed commission dropped the hearings. No one was prosecuted for the crimes and abuses listed in our statement. The federal and state authorities sat on the evidence. Instead of court action, letters streamed into the editors of the state newspapers denying that discrimination against the Indian was ever practiced by a white South Dakotan. A good many of them took the opportunity to attack me personally. Other letters were honest: they just said that the Indian should keep his mouth shut. My mother received two letters threatening her; they stated that she should keep her "squaw" mouth shut, and one had attached to it a strip of cellophane tape. This had a clear fingerprint, which we turned over to the federal authorities. Peter Pitchlynn, a special officer of

---

* "The Impact on State Jurisdiction upon Assuming Jurisdiction over Indians." Professor William Farber, University of South Dakota, 1958.

the BIA, managed to "lose" the evidence. We were clearly getting a runaround, and many of my original supporters were beginning to lose interest, but I was determined to see the issue through.

Then, as if in answer to my prayers, Donald Janson, a reporter from *The New York Times*, arrived in South Dakota. Janson came to my office, where I reviewed my testimony and the evidence we had gathered for the congressional committee, as well as what had been going on in South Dakota since the subject first hit the newspapers. We drove over to the town of Martin, where I had known the city police chief to chain Indian men by their ankles to the jail bunks. A chain and the attached padlock once had been smuggled out of jail and placed on the rear seat of my car while I had been inside talking to the prisoners. I had seen forty-two prisoners crammed into a filthy, reeking cell that was intended to hold eight. I told Janson of these observations on the way to the town.

The reporter's first story was an interview with the chief of police of Martin. In the interview Janson quoted the chief as saying, "These Indians are like niggers in the south, give them a break and they will take over." The situation was receiving national news coverage, and I wondered what the self-righteous South Dakotans who had cried so loudly that no discrimination existed in their state were thinking now.

For the next three years the state officials did everything in their power to forestall any investigation into the facts disclosed by *The New York Times*. The brutal law enforcement officers who had been guilty of abuses listed in my report continued to act with impunity. In Winner, South Dakota, a state patrolman walked into the city jail and fired his tear gas gun into the cells where Indian men and women were imprisoned. "Tell your chairman, Burnette, about this and see what he can do about it," he told them. In Todd County, law officers passed jail keys around to police and nonpolice alike. Members of this "key" club entered the cells of Indian women and raped them. In another incident, the police loosed a police dog on six Indian men in a cell.

While the country was outraged by the reports, South Dakota did nothing—except to smother the issue by indifference and outright evasion. The only thing that seemed important to the people of South Dakota was that a picture of tranquil relations between Indians and whites be portrayed; because of this, the Indians who dared to complain about discrimination were even more savagely reminded that they were without rights and at the complete mercy of the whites.

We turned our attention to the processing of the loan application. Everything was in order and the application was sent to Roger Ernst. On December 10, 1959, we learned that Ernst had approved our $500,000 loan and our fifteen-year land utilization program, which was to be funded by the loan.

A new election was coming up in January 1960, but I expected little opposition to our administration in view of the solid gains we had made for the tribe. Again, I went to a Sioux religious ceremony, and again the outcome of the election was predicted—I was to win, unopposed, by twenty-two votes. As before, I was reelected councilman from the Swift Bear community and president of the Rosebud Sioux Tribal Council—by twenty-two votes.

Nineteen-sixty passed uneventfully, and we pressed ahead to our long-range goals. During this year I became interested in organizations that appeared to represent the national interests of the Indian. I discovered that most of these organizations—there are more than a hundred of them—which are, in large, run and joined by non-Indians, did less than nothing to help the Indian, on whose behalf they were constantly raising money. I estimated that over two million dollars, raised from the general public, passes into the hands of people who have little or no intention of assisting the Indian. For example, the Association on American Indian Affairs has raised hundreds of thousands of dollars, of which it expends 10 to 15 percent on matters directly affecting Indians on reservations. Until very recently, the Association would not allow any Indian on their board of directors. In 1962 and 1963 the legal counsel of the Association testified in favor of the "Heirship Bill,"* which would have brought destruction to the Indian as surely as termination.

The tribes opposed this proposed legislation, first, because it is

* See Appendix.

67

unconstitutional to sell property without the consent of the owners; second, because land sales could be made for as little as 75 percent of the actual value of the land; third, because once this act became law, the BIA would forget about the provision under which Indians and the total tribe were protected. We also knew that congress would never appropriate money enough to meet the needs of all the tribes concerned. We had been fooled by treaties before, so we were not to be fooled again by a figure set forth in a bill in congress.

Time and time again the Association on American Indian Affairs and other so-called Indian organizations would take a position diametrically opposed to that of the Indians—another example of the non-Indian knowing what's best for the Indian. Most galling, at least three quarters of the money people contribute to these organizations under the impression that they are helping the Indian goes right into salaries, office expenses, and the like.

Some few organizations did help the Indians; still we needed a national outfit that would represent all Indians. The National Congress of American Indians fulfilled this need, functioning as the Indians' "lobby" in Washington. In September of 1961 the tribe delegated me to attend the annual convention of the National Congress of American Indians, in Lewiston, Idaho. I had been active for some time in a campaign to encourage Indian leadership on the national level, and to my surprise the leaders of the thirty-seven tribes attending the convention asked me to take the executive directorship of the NCAI and move to Washington. They promised to give the NCAI support—including financial support—if I would accept the offer. My immediate reaction was that here was the chance of a lifetime to help all Indian people by representing them strongly and honestly in Washington. I told them that if my tribe, through the council, would release me from the presidency I would accept the position.

When I returned to the reservation some of the councilmen and tribe members advised me to stay on as president; they feared the tribal government would descend into the corruption and indifference that characterized it before the younger men and I had first been elected to tribal office. But most of the tribe thought it would be a splendid move for me, and that I could benefit the Indian cause across the nation.

I took the question to the council, and asked them to decide whether I should stay or go to Washington. Cato Valandra, a councilman from St. Francis, made a motion to pay my salary in advance up to January 26, 1962, and let me take the NCAI job. The motion was passed unanimously.

My family and I left for Washington on November 17, 1961. I looked forward to working with John F. Kennedy's administration; at the same time I had an uneasy feeling that all would not be well with my tribe. Within three short years, I would be back on Rosebud, beginning the fight, again, against corrupt federal and tribal forces.

Why has so little material progress
been made on Indian reservations?
Just how do tribal leaders exploit
and the Bureau of Indian Affairs
stifle the Indian people? Why can't
something be done about it? I asked
these questions and lived the answers.
This book is witness to two decades
in the lives of ten thousand Rosebud
Sioux Indians—and representative of
the experience of reservations around
the country. It documents the fight
of a few against the forces of an evil
status quo. It is an answer to the
ignorant white man who asks me,
"How big a check does the government give you every month?" It is an
answer to the Indian politico and the
BIA official who ask me not to make
trouble, reminding me that I, too,
could be a smart Indian, a rich Indian,
a corrupt Indian. It is a record that I
hope will work a change. . . .
                    —Robert Burnette

Fraud, graft, corruption, and murder
are recurrent themes in this telling of
the story of the American Indian's long
and courageous struggle for freedom
and equality in his native land. *The
Tortured Americans*, written by an
American Indian, describes the
agonies and hardships endured by
the first Americans today, and chal-
lenges the American conscience to
action.

k office in Washington at the National
gress of American Indians on December
'61. The first few days were not aus-
us. I learned immediately that the out-
staff and director had stripped the
and that the simple business of getting
t as much of a battle as securing rights

d the responsibility to protect the In-
ished to destroy our land base. With-
was finished. As long as he had land,
his standard of living, for forming a
d serve each individual member, for

a legislative watchdog. On paper it
anization, but lack of support—par-
y crippled its activities. The tribes
their interests, but they were not as
he necessary financial support. As a
es I was to encounter, attorneys' fees
4 would run to one million dollars
contribution totaled approximately

ces, I felt the organization could still
do a job, by getting to influential politicians, making them aware of
Indian interests, and working to gain political support and sym-
pathy. I was able to get a good start when Bernard Cherin, who had
worked in the Kennedy campaign and whom I had met in Sioux
Falls in 1960, contacted me. As a freelance representative of the
Kennedy administration, he wanted first-hand information on In-

dian problems, which had attracted Kennedy's interest. With his help I was able to meet people who were in a position to aid the Indian's cause, and to be alerted of important meetings regarding Indian matters. He became a good friend, and his advice and help, especially to a reservation Indian newly arrived in a city of two million people after the spacious plains of South Dakota, was inestimable.

In May 1962 the controversy begun by my testimony before congress back in 1959 boiled up again. The state attorney general's office announced that a John Doe hearing would be held in the Justice of the Peace's Court in Winner, South Dakota, the scene of some of the alleged criminal acts against Indians. The new tribal chairman, Cato Valandra, did not offer me the necessary money so I could come home for the hearing, and the NCAI was completely without funds, so I sat helplessly in Washington, listening to reports of the hearing as it proceeded. Many of the witnesses to acts against Indians disappeared. Others who did appear at the hearing were harassed and discredited by the investigating authorities. But a good number of witnesses endured the abuse and held to their stories.

My absence hurt the Indian cause, and I was to become even more disheartened when I learned that, although the hearing was ostensibly held to gather evidence that would lead to an indictment of the guilty law officers, in fact the attorney general was seeking evidence that would make possible an indictment of *me* on some charge. Two days after the hearing concluded, persons from my tribe began to write me, telling of payoffs to important witnesses. One young lady received seven hundred dollars to leave the county. (She was later killed by an automobile on a wide street in Black Hills, and the city officials had her embalmed without notifying her kin or ordering an inquest; the driver of the auto that hit her went free.) I also heard from my tribe that the new tribal leaders were not protecting the tribe's interests and were attempting to discredit my performance as Executive Director.

I decided to take the issue to Robert F. Kennedy, the attorney general. He received me, and listened to my detailed report on the incidents and the hearings of the past couple of years. He was visibly angered when informed of the actions of the so-called law enforcement officers. He told me that his office would do all that was possible to investigate the affair; but that as long as the state continued with its investigations, the federal authorities could do nothing. I knew that the state authorities were stalling for time, as eventually the duration set by the statute of limitations would be reached and offenders would be beyond prosecution. It was interesting to observe that none of the accused brought civil action against us for slander or libel. They knew that if they did, we would have the opportunity to prove the truth of our charges.

Meanwhile, congress had set up a new subcommittee, the Subcommittee on the Constitutional Rights of the American Indians, which was investigating the lack of such rights. I discussed the relevant developments in my area of South Dakota with Senator Sam Ervin, Jr., and the subcommittee announced that it would hold hearings in Pierre, South Dakota, and Bismarck, North Dakota, during June of 1962.

I borrowed five hundred dollars and traveled home to attend the hearings. Hundreds of Indians from South Dakota came forward to testify at the Pierre hearing. The Oglala Sioux testified against the police chief of Martin. One witness related that two city officers beat him while his hands were handcuffed behind his back. His front teeth had been smashed from his mouth by their nightsticks, and because the police could not knock him to the ground, the chief of police fired his tear gas gun point blank into the man's face, breaking his jaw and temporarily blinding him. A near riot developed, and the man escaped into the crowd. His testimony was confirmed by others who had been present at the incident. Indian women from Martin testified how they had been beaten when arrested and reported the use of ankle chains to bind prisoners in the jail cells. Scores of Indian witnesses submitted evidence of police brutality, wisely bringing with them witnesses who could confirm their testimony. I submitted affidavits from Indian victims of police abuse. The subcommittee gathered a great deal of damning evi-

73

dence, which was printed in a three volume report on the hearing available to the general public.*

The matter did not rest there. In August of the following year, 1963, the South Dakota authorities chose to hold another John Doe hearing. I was summoned to the court to prove charges that were by then more than five years old. I accepted the challenge and appeared in court with thirty-two witnesses. The hearing was worse than a farce; it was an outright attempt to intimidate me and all Indians who might complain about treatment received at the hands of the law. The statute of limitations had run out, and all of the accused had successfully avoided any consequences for their actions. These men were present in the courtroom. One of them, pointed out by three witnesses as the perpetrator of a crime, had been appointed bailiff, and stood before the witnesses armed with a .38 pistol. When I took the witness stand, I was attacked for having shamed the state. I had the frightening feeling of being in a foreign country, without rights, before a kangaroo court. Each witness was harassed; questions were twisted in an attempt to make the witness waver from the truth; but regardless of the intimidation and innuendo (the witnesses were asked how much money I had given them to testify) we all stuck to the facts. At noon, the court recessed. I called the press to tell them we were going home, disregarding the summons issued by the court. When we left, the officials did nothing to stop us. They felt they had accomplished their purpose.

I was proud of my people, who had not budged in the face of considerable threats posed by the white authorities. When you are without rights or power, it is not easy to stand up to those who you know can revenge themselves on you with impunity. I was sick of the bullying and hypocrisy of the whites, people elected to protect each citizen and appointed to enforce laws fairly. I was reminded of a mural that hung on the wall in the governor's office; it depicted a white man dressed in buckskin, a long-rifle in his

* Hearings before the Subcommittee on Constitutional Rights of the Committee on the Judiciary, U.S. Senate. 87th Congress, First Session, Part 1, Part 2, Part 3.

74

hands, standing with his left foot on the head of an Indian corpse. A wagon train was in the background, and scattered about it were dead Sioux warriors. It was entitled "The Spirit of South Dakota." That spirit had certainly survived pioneer times and was alive and well in the atomic age.

The final outcome of our long and humiliating fight for justice under law was the natural death by indifference of the issues. No one was indicted; no responsibility for the disgraceful acts committed was ever assumed. But bit by bit, month by month, we did accomplish some change. The law officers involved were eventually relieved of their positions, and the wholesale arrest of Indians slowed to at least a retail rate. By April 1964 we could recognize the difference; our old enemies were gone, and the state court system had improved significantly in its handling of Indian cases. And most heartening, the people of South Dakota defeated a proposed law which sought to take state jurisdiction over Indian reservations. The vote was 4 to 1 in our favor.

My first year as director of the NCAI, 1962, passed quickly. I had begun to lay the foundation on which a fortress to protect Indian interests could be raised. I had attended hundreds of meetings on subjects of importance to Indians; I had met with congressmen on a score of Indian matters. Cherin and I had gone to Presidential committee meetings, chaired by Vice-President Lyndon B. Johnson. I was able to meet and speak to people who could vitally affect the American Indian. That year I had talks with Hubert Humphrey, Averell Harriman, Angier Biddle Duke, Robert F. Kennedy, Bernard Bernhardt, and Laurance Rockefeller.

It wasn't long before the NCAI's worth was tested. Again the Heirship Bill was introduced into Congress. (How tired the Indians get fighting off the same threats; one would think the whites would similarly tire of working on the same plan to acquire Indian land.) A friend furnished me with a copy of the proposed legislation, and we had time to plan its defeat. It contained the same provisions as before: termination of federal services to the reservations, restriction of the number of Indians who could inherit property, and the power to take Indian land without compensation. We knew that termination of federal services would wreak havoc on the reservations; but also the local, and therefore the state, economy would be damaged. And it probably meant that some 55 million acres of land would be placed on the auction block and millions of acres of timber land would be sold, thus inflating an already strained element of the economy, upon which many Indians depended for their livelihood. If Indian lands were taxed, it was easy to see what would happen to the land of those Indians—a majority certainly—who were ignorant of local tax laws.

We began working to defeat this measure. I called all the tribes and asked them to send delegates into the capital to show their opposition to the bill. We needed newspaper coverage that would present our side of the case to the public. We interested a reporter on the Washington *Post* in the story, and he interviewed Dolly Akers, Donald Deernose, and myself in the preparation of an article reporting the Indian's point of view. In an act of desperation, I called Evelyn Dubrow, lobbyist for David Dubinsky's International Ladies Garment Workers' Union, and asked to talk to her. After hearing me out on what I considered to be potentially the biggest land steal of the century, she consented to take my message directly to President Kennedy. The day before the hearing, we invited James Gamble, the Indian Committee adviser, to present his interpretation of the bill to the executive council, which included a member of every tribe in the nation. Gamble had pursued the course of termination unflaggingly, and we thought it would not only be fair to hear the opposition's principal exponent discuss the bill, but it would be psychologically useful to have confronted the opposition. Gamble agreed to speak, on the condition that no questions be asked. He gave his comments on the bill and left the meeting amid silence.

We had marshaled our forces, and yet I had no reason to hope we could defeat the proposal. It was such an age-old procedure—a promise or a treaty, then a broken promise or treaty, and then a new promise or a treaty that would soon be broken. The whites were unswerving in dedication to relieving the Indian of anything they consider valuable. I was reminded of a story about an Indian,

Little White Cloud, who accompanied a delegation to Washington to make a settlement with white BIA officials for Indian land that was taken so that a huge dam could be built on it. The Indian commissioner greeted the delegation warmly, and wined and dined them in preparation for the signing of documents which would give the tribe minimum compensation for their land. They ordered steaks all around, and the commissioner watched as Little White Cloud devoured his meal. "Mr. Little White Cloud," the commissioner said, jovially, "I wish I had your appetite so that I could enjoy a meal as you do." Little White Cloud replied, "Mr. Commissioner, you government people have taken all my Black Hills gold, all my land, you've taken my children from home and away to school, you've taken most of my reservation, and now you want the only thing I have left to enjoy. You want to take away my appetite."

But we did have hope. There is an Indian proverb which says that there will be Indians in this country (South Dakota) so long as there is water in the land. And, indeed, for all the disasters that befell us, we are still there.

On March 8, 1963, the hearing for this new version of the Heirship Bill was held in Washington. The room was filled by more than a hundred anxious Indians, and a large number of white men, quite conspicuously wearing cowboy hats. Sometime after 9:00 A.M. a man entered the hearing room and whispered something to the white men sitting in the last row of seats. They, in turn, relayed the word down to the front of the room. The "cowboys" rose and filed out of the room. I figured that the bill was assured of passage, and that the obviously prepared witnesses had been told their services would not be needed. A few minutes later, Senator Lee Metcalf of Montana asked to see me. In his office he told me that the Heirship Bill was dead. President Kennedy had urged the senators to kill the proposed legislation in the committee, and his wishes had been respected. I knew why the men had left the room so hurriedly; they were preparing another version of the bill, after deleting certain provisions.

This new bill, watered down but still poisonous in the view of the Indian, was discussed in the hearing room. I made a prepared statement on behalf of the NCAI. When I had finished, the Demo-

77

cratic senator from New Mexico, Clinton Anderson,* asked me if I had ever heard the comment that he and Senator Gordon Allot were the greatest enemies the Indians ever had? I can only guess that he was trying to intimidate me by such a question, but I said, yes, I'd heard such a comment on several occasions, in the company of Indians. He did not become angry, as I had expected, but remarked that Allot was a good attorney and that he had always taken care of "his" Indians. It was men like Anderson, whose interests were directly opposed to that of the Indians, and who were powerful enough to influence legislation regarding Indians, who blocked much of the legislation that would benefit our people and supported legislation detrimental to us.

The day after the hearing, the Washington *Post* ran a half-page story quoting Dolly Akers and Donald Deernose, who revealed the uglier aspects of this anti-Indian bill. The story hit the streets just as another hearing on the bill was scheduled to be held. Luckily, Kennedy intervened once again, and this version—one could call it the March 1963 Heirship Bill—was sunk. The Indian could relax until a new version surfaced.

The executive council had met during the hearings, and my glumness over the proposed legislation was deepened by my financial state. I had exactly fifty cents to my name to feed my family. The NCAI was broke. On top of this, I was growing increasingly depressed by the Washington atmosphere. I saw very clearly that the principles of liberty and justice were just a schoolboy's lesson, and that the practical process of government pivoted on one's social and political status, on whom one knew, and on how much one could contribute. I thought of my experiences, of Washington's social circles, attending rounds of parties which, I had thought, would

---

* Anderson's interests in the National Forest Service, and banking, timber, uranium, and other industries in his home state often brought him into conflict with Indian demands. An exchange with Paul Bernal, a Toos Pueblo Indian, over land considered sacred by Bernal's tribe, illustrates Anderson's attitude. "I [Bernal] said to Senator Anderson: 'Why do you want to steal our sacred land?'

"Senator Anderson said: 'Paul, I like you. But there is timber on that land, millions of dollars of timber.'" From *Our Brother's Keeper*, ed. Edgar S. Cahn (Washington, D.C., 1969). Quotation is from 25 U.S.C. § 2 (1968).

provide a fine opportunity to talk to different politicians about the American Indian. I was disgusted by the boasting, the vulgarity, the drunkenness of people who are supposed to be the leaders of the country. On many occasions I watched members of congress stagger about, benumbed by alcohol. It afforded me little satisfaction to see prestigious whites, fallen prey to their own poison, which had tragically ruined so many Indian lives.

I appealed to the nation's tribes to support the NCAI, which had substantially contributed to the defeat of the Heirship Bill, thereby saving some 55 million acres of Indian land. The Standing Rock Sioux generously responded with a donation of $5,000, and challenged the other tribes to make similar pledges. Unfortunately, the tribes, who could not see the forest for their own few trees, did not promise any support. The NCAI was still tottering on the edge of bankruptcy. It was doubly unfortunate, for we were, through the NCAI, receiving recognition and respect from the men who could help us most. A few days before the hearings on the Heirship Bill, at my suggestion, President Kennedy had welcomed 104 tribal leaders to the White House.

Although the prospects of the NCAI were dimmed by financial problems, the nation's Indians enjoyed a few months respite from threatening legislation and basked in the sudden interest some of the country's leaders were showing for them. Then in late 1963, as surely as the sun rises, another Heirship Bill was introduced into Congress. This time, lulled perhaps by former victories, the tribes did not respond to the alarm. Only the Crow, the Colorado River, the Standing Rock Sioux, and the Cheyenne River Sioux tribes came to Washington to protect their interests. Our weak protests were in vain, and an amended version of the Heirship Bill passed the Senate. Our only hope was to convince the House Indian Affairs Committee that the proposed legislation would seriously damage the American Indian. Exactly ten Indians went to see James Haley, chairman of the Indian subcommittee. He listened to us and made a fair suggestion. He advised us to have all the tribes contribute to a proposal that could be introduced in Congress as the Indians' answer to the Heirship Bill. We left with a one-year respite in which to develop a counter-proposal.

Early in November 1963 I borrowed a thousand dollars for expenses and began a trip that would take me through almost every Indian area in the nation. I looked forward to the trip with enormous enthusiasm. I would be in the open again, breathing fresh air and seeing the land as it had been throughout the tens of thousands of years of my people's history. I went through North Dakota, South Dakota, Montana, Washington, Oregon, California, and stopped to rest in Arizona, where a meeting of the Arizona tribes was scheduled in Parker, the home of the Mohave Indians.

We had planned a thorough discussion of land problems and, in the dry southwest, the inevitable concomitant, water problems. After the first morning's talks, we broke for lunch, and that afternoon, November 22, 1963, heard the incredible news that President Kennedy had been shot. We huddled around the radio until the tragic news of his death was reported. We were particularly saddened by the death of this president, for he had been most responsive to Indian needs. It was a day of dreadful loss to us.

I suggested we adjourn the meeting and return to our homes. The following day I drove toward Washington on the widest, loneliest road I ever saw. It seemed that everyone was home or at church, and each town and city I passed through seemed to be in mourning. I traveled over eight hundred miles that day and did not see more than fifty cars on the road.

I arrived in Washington after the funeral, and it seemed a month passed before the numbness of the awful tragedy wore away. I contacted the Secretary of the Interior, Stewart Udall, for an appointment, and hoped eventually for a meeting with President Johnson. The meeting with Udall was a good one, and he helped to set up a date in January on which the President would see the tribal leaders.

On January 18, 1964, several days before the planned meeting with the President, Walter Wetzel, NCAI president, convened the executive council. The meeting of the NCAI promised to be well attended, not only by member Indians, but by such interested persons as Doris Duke, Marlon Brando, and Eugene Burdick. Their presence brought welcome publicity to the Indian cause.

Clyde Warrior, a Ponca Indian from Oklahoma (who had the

80

reputation of being the "Stokely Carmichael of the Indians") issued a strong challenge to the older tribal leaders. He chose to avoid the back-patting and hand-shaking form of address, and instead blasted the leaders for their failure to protect and represent their people. He angrily told the gathering of leaders that they had not accomplished a thing for the Indian. The conference had begun with fireworks.

I agreed with Warrior's remarks; in fact, I had wanted to say some of the same things for the past three years. But I disagreed with the manner in which he assaulted the leaders in the plainest of language before our guests and the Indian women. Warrior was to agree with me that he had been intemperate in the words he chose; but I was pleased that a more militant stance had been proposed. Now, perhaps, the Indian leaders could get together, and not benefit the BIA by their bickering and procrastination. The spirit of the meeting was that there was everything to gain and nothing to lose, so we proceeded to separate the men from the boys —that is, to separate the pro-BIA, Uncle Tom-a-hawk Indians from the anti-BIA forces who stood for tough and autonomous Indian leadership.

I appealed to the delegates for unity, and proposed, as a concrete example of our purpose, that each tribe contribute to a war chest that would assist all Indians in the fight to control their own destinies. I urged that this fund be used for loans to Indians, and that the sum be $200 million. Such a source of money would be vital to Indians, who cannot legally borrow money without the BIA's approval. Not only would it help individuals and tribes who before had no means of credit, but it would remove the Indian a step from the shadow of the BIA, and give him a measure of autonomy.

I saw the delegates who owed their political lives to the BIA shrink at this proposal. I told the delegates that I hoped they would pass a resolution establishing just such a fund. I told them that I envisioned Congress enacting new laws that would make it possible for an individual Indian to defend himself within the structure of tribal government, laws that would make all Indians holding public tribal positions accountable to the members of their tribe, and laws that would enable an Indian to enter the federal courts if the

81

tribal court system failed to satisfy his quest for justice. I tried to underscore the principle that was at stake, a principle that had been indicated by Clyde Warrior: that we as Indians must assume control over our lives, so long dominated by agencies of the United States, and by corrupt, traitorous Indian leaders; that we must achieve our own destiny, economically and culturally.

The response to my speech was enthusiastic; I did not believe that what I had suggested was more than a dream at that time, but I hoped to see the beginnings of that dream come true.

On January 20, 1964, we met with President Johnson. It was a historic occasion for the Indian; we would have had two meetings with a President of the United States in the space of one year. After a visit to the Kennedy grave, we were ushered into the East Wing of the White House. When Johnson arrived he greeted every delegate; he listened as Walter Wetzel talked about the policies of the NCAI, and asked him what the future might hold for Indian relations with the federal government. The President assured us that the Indian policies of the Kennedy administration would be pursued, and that he would push for the appropriations needed for important Indian programs. The meeting was polite and the talk optimistic; but I did not feel the Kennedy warmth, and suspected the President's interest was motivated by political considerations rather than by a concern for Indian problems.

Shortly after our executive council conference, we had a signal success in a battle with the BIA. During the conference the Colorado River tribes reported that they had had a $2,080,000 land improvement lease bid rejected by the BIA, even though it was the highest amount bid on the land they wanted to lease. Word had it that the rejection was due to pressure from a Texas based corporation which was interested in the land but did not want to top the bid of Bruce Church, Inc. I felt the White House might have supplied a little muscle in getting the BIA to disapprove of the projected lease, so I asked Pete Homer, chairman of the tribe, to fly the corporation officials who had made the high bid to Washington. I then instructed the tribe to forward to Senators Barry Goldwater and Carl Hayden a resolution from the tribe approving the bid. One morning Pete Homer, the corporation officials, and I went to the department of the interior office and told the BIA people that we were going to fight to have the bid—which met all legal requirements and had been approved by the tribe—okayed by the BIA. We were sent from one office to another, and we told the harried-looking BIA officials we were prepared to go to Congress if they denied us satisfaction. Within an hour, an assistant Commissioner of Indian Affairs informed me that the Bureau had reconsidered and now approved the bid.

Pete Homer flew home, a happy man. His tribe was richer by $2,080,000, and 6,500 acres of sandy desert would soon be a permanent income-producing asset to the tribe, creating employment for tribal members.

On January 21, 1964, I informed several of the NCAI people of my decision to resign my position of executive director. I did not reveal my reasons to them. Since the previous year I had been learning that conditions on my Rosebud reservation had become grotesquely bad. I could hardly believe some of the reports that filtered back to me of abuses by tribal leaders. I knew I had to return and try to correct a situation for which I felt partly responsible. I planned to leave the NCAI in July 1964; I would use a bit of my remaining time at the organization to check out more closely the facts about the Rosebud reservation.

5
Starting
Over in Rosebud

The first inkling of trouble on my reservation had occurred back in the spring of
1963, at a meeting with Graham Holmes,
who was then Assistant Commissioner of
Indian Affairs. We chatted about general
matters, and Holmes finally asked me if I had heard of the Blue
Thunder land deal on Rosebud. I said no, and he explained that
someone had purchased a woman's land improperly, but that it had
been caught by the BIA. Later that year, in the fall, a Rosebud
councilman hinted to me about a land case. I ignored the implica-
tion, thinking that the problem had been satisfactorily resolved.

Other reports and rumors had come to my attention, and led in
January 1964 to my decision to resign from the NCAI and return
to Rosebud. As word got to the NCAI members that I would be
leaving, several tried to convince me to stay. I could only tell them
that I felt responsible for a worsening situation at home, and that I
must return and make an attempt to correct it. One of the federal
employees at the Rosebud Agency was there only because Roger
Ernst, Assistant Secretary of the Interior, asked me to make a man
of this bureaucrat—Harold W. Schunk. Schunk was an Indian, and
I agreed to let him give the job a try. Another man, Cato Valandra,
now president of the tribe, had served under me for a number of
years and had gained my trust. Now I was receiving reports that
he and Schunk were damaging the tribe: Valandra had illegally
mortgaged tribal cattle, illegally indebted the tribe in two states,
defrauded the people of money and lands, and a clique of Valandra's relatives were using the power of his office to their own ends.
I had to return to investigate these allegations. It seemed that in the
few years that I had been gone, two wicked but powerful men had
gained control of everything on the Rosebud reservation, including the law enforcement personnel. If an Indian protested some act

of theirs, the individual was simply cut off from his own money. The two men, from what I had heard, were truly little "Hitlers," and the poor tribesmen had no way of remedying the situation under the United States laws which bound them.

Then in March 1964 a delegation from the Sioux tribes came to Washington to raise funds to fight the state's Republican forces, which were backing legislation that would give the state full jurisdiction over the nine tribes. They called upon me for aid, and I took them to interested people who might contribute money to their cause. While we were working on fund-raising, I received a visit from one of our tribal officials. He invited me and my secretary out to dinner. I knew something strange was going on, and decided that this would be a good opportunity to find out exactly what. My secretary and I met the man and a companion of his at his motel, and before I had time to order a cocktail he was reviewing my entire career. He summed up by telling me, "Burnette, you have worked for more than ten years for the Indians and you haven't received anything for your work except a kick in the ass. . . . Wise up, make money while you still can, because those damn Indians don't appreciate your work. Forget them and join us." He turned to his companion from the Standing Rock Sioux tribe, and continued, "I am making money on everything that crosses my desk and you are making money on what you do, ain't that right, pal?" The man agreed. Rosebud's official came to the point: "Burnette, I want you to come back home and take over TLE and we will get rich together. With your brains and know-how, we can own the Rosebud Reservation in five years. Think it over and let me know. How about it?"

I was dumbfounded. This was a man I had once trusted and supported. But he was giving me a superb opportunity to gather damning evidence against him and his cohorts. I asked for time to think it over. My secretary was looking at me with murder in her eyes. I told the man to give me time to clean up NCAI business, as I was planning to resign my position. I would give him my answer in July. He accepted happily, as if I had just signed a pact with the devil.

On the way back from the motel, my secretary raged about Indians who broke faith with their people, as I began planning my strategy for this man's removal and for my investigation of conditions at Rosebud. I hoped that I would discover that this meeting had been nothing but boasting, but I knew in my bones what I would uncover when I returned home.

Shortly afterward I had a chance to visit Rosebud. I went to see those individuals who would be able to give me a truthful report on the activities of the tribal government. A councilman who had served with me for six years confirmed my worst fears. He gave me a list of the names of people who had lost large amounts of money in land transactions with the tribal officials. I learned that friends and relatives of the tribal officials were purchasing Tribal Land Enterprise certificates for less than half their true value. And this was going on under the direct supervision of the BIA and its superintendent. I could not believe the BIA would involve itself in fraud, and yet the facts were incontrovertible. I found documented evidence that tribal officers were issuing purchase orders to tribespeople in lieu of cash for the TLE certificates. There were actually hundreds of such illegal letters of guarantee, called purchase orders, issued in violation of federal laws. I found out that the tribal calf crop, from excellent stock cows, was being diverted to the herds of relatives of the tribal officers. I also learned that a large mortgage had been drawn against 670 head of tribal cattle by the Nebraska State Bank of Valentine, Nebraska, and that the mortgage money was unaccounted for.

I was stunned. This information came out in one afternoon. It was clear that the offer made to me that promised ownership of the reservation in several years was based on a solid conspiratorial foundation.

I returned to Washington, and formulated my plans to expose and prosecute those people who were so ruthlessly abusing their office and exploiting their own people. At the same time I still had NCAI commitments to carry out. A national conference was planned for May 1964 to publicize the extreme poverty of America's Indians. Good friends of the Indian—Rev. Clifford Samuelson of the National Council of the Episcopal Church, Mrs. Betty Josephy, Mrs. Betty Clark Rosenthal, Lawrence E. Lindley, executive director of the Indian Rights Association—all helped to develop the program.

The conference began successfully on May 9, and ran for four days. Hubert H. Humphrey delivered the keynote address, "Poverty in Our National Life," and I spoke on poverty in Indian life. During the following days we had a gathering at the National Cathedral on Wisconsin Avenue to dramatize the plight of the American Indian, and the NCAI sponsored a program of Indian arts and culture, at which Alvin M. Josephy, an editor of *American Heritage* magazine and author of several books on Indians, spoke about the many contributions to American culture made by the Indian.

The program was highlighted by a congressional reception held in the United States Capitol Building, attended by a number of congressmen and senators. Indian delegates had the opportunity to impress these lawmakers with the dire needs that exist on every reservation. They seized the opportunity and discussed with the legislators such problems as a 90 percent national unemployment rate among Indians, a death rate double that of the national average, an educational level that averaged the completion of seven grades. Many of the senators and congressmen may have learned these facts for the first time. They also learned that housing conditions among Indians were deplorable and that discrimination against Indians was rampant; that in 1964, 8,000 Indian children did not attend school because there was no classroom space for them; that thousands of Indians went hungry and more survived only on surplus food, mostly starches; that health conditions were on an emergency level; that a large number of Indians lived in automobile bodies and in ragged tents. There was probably more communication that afternoon between American Indians and American lawmakers than had taken place in the world's history. The conference ended on May 12 and we thought it had been a resounding success. Our conclusion was borne out when Indians were included in the legislation that created the "War Against Poverty."

The only discordant note in the conference was sounded by the Association on American Indian Affairs. The executive director, Bill Byler, refused to allow his organization to take part in the poverty conference because he wanted a conference on education. This kind of backbiting among organizations supposedly dedicated to the welfare of Indians was galling; but what griped me even more was that the NCAI, which worked so hard on behalf of the Indian tribes, was constantly hampered by lack of funds while such organizations as the Association are by comparison rich. A major part of the budget of these organizations goes to professional fund-raisers, staff salaries, and equipment expenses. These contributions could have been put to direct use in helping the Indian by the NCAI, the United Scholarship Service Incorporated of Denver, Colorado, the Indian Rights Association, and the various church groups that sincerely and legitimately represent the Indian's interests. I was to have run-ins with Byler, whose Association on Indian Affairs was, of course, all white, and therefore supposed it knew what was best for the Indian. Time that could have been better spent directly on Indian matters had to be devoted to finding out what other "Indian" organizations were doing; if their activities were dangerous, as in the instance when the Association supported the Heirship Bill in opposition to the wishes of the Indian tribes, then more time and labor had to be invested in what must have seemed to outsiders as debilitating internecine warfare.

My troubles at this time were compounded by other absurdities. I had been working on the proposed Civil Rights Act of 1964, and had met with various Negro leaders. Some Indians did not want to associate themselves with the black cause. It seemed logical to me to ally ourselves with another minority's determination to obtain their rights, but I guess that fear or prejudice can affect an Indian's mind as well as a white's. So telephone calls would come into my office from Indians who wished to criticize my interest in the bill and my meetings with black leaders. However, I approached Senator Humphrey, as I had planned, and requested that the Civil Rights Act be amended by the insertion of the words "Indian Tribes" at a strategic place in the bill, so that the tribes would be able to control fully the employment practices on Indian reservations. Humphrey suggested I speak to Senator Karl Mundt from South Dakota. Mundt agreed to sponsor the amendment and it was duly passed into law. The amazing conclusion to this matter is that,

89

to my knowledge, not one single tribe has used this law to benefit unemployed Indians. I knew of many instances in which it could have been utilized to advantage, but the tribal leadership chose to ignore the Indian provisions of the act.

Early in June I traveled out to Montana on NCAI business. I planned to visit Rosebud on my way back to Washington. I stopped by Donald Deernose's house in Lodge Grass, Montana, and Donald cheered me up with a wonderful story. It got me to thinking that even if the white man managed to take away the Indian's appetite, the Indian's sense of humor would still be safe. It is an indissoluble part of each Indian's heritage and gives him sustenance when times are grim—as they often are for the Indian.

Donald told me of an old Crow Indian (Donald and his wife are Montana Crows) named John. He drove a team of two white mares, one a small horse, the other a great big one, wherever he went. A neighboring white rancher owned a perfect match for the larger horse, and he had been trying for some time to buy the mare cheaply. One day the rancher decided that he would own that horse before the sun set, and he drove over to the reservation. He found John driving along the road. He stopped the Indian and offered him $250 for the mare. John said, "I no sellum, she don't look so good." The rancher offered $300. John replied, "I no sellum, she don't look so good." The rancher desperately raised his offer to $350. John said, "You wantum bad so I sellum, but she don't look so good." The rancher thought he had skinned another Indian, and he tied the mare to the tailgate of his truck. When he arrived at his ranch, he led the horse to the barn, but it ran right into the wall, missing the doorway. The rancher waved his hand in front of the mare's face and found that she was totally blind. He raged and cursed the damn Indian for beating him out of $350. So he tied the horse to his pickup and rushed back to where John was struggling with a one-horse hitch to his wagon. He demanded the return of his money because John had failed to tell him that the horse was blind. John said calmly, "I told you, she don't look so good," and drove away in his one-horse hitch.

The next day I headed toward Rosebud, now feeling terribly anxious about how I would fight the powerful group that had corrupted the Rosebud reservation. I thought that going along with the gang might give me a chance to gather the evidence I needed, but the danger that I might have to involve myself in their activities in order to carry off the masquerade was too great. I decided to fight them in the open, to buck "city hall."

Early the next morning, after my arrival at Rosebud, I visited with some of the councilmen. It was easy to see that they were disturbed, but evidently each man felt he stood alone, and therefore was powerless to protest the corrupt leadership. My old friend, Jesse Good Voice, told me privately, in the Sioux language, of the rotten land deals, the illegal purchase orders, and the officials whose predilection for thievery ran in their backgrounds through several generations. I told Jesse that I must have solid written evidence of wrongdoing before I could act.

Mr. and Mrs. Henry Big Crow told me similar stories of extortion and fraud. One transaction, that of Joe Kills The Enemy, was familiar to me, for I had been the tribal negotiator in the sale of his land to the tribe. It was excruciating to find that people whom I had dealt with in good faith had fallen prey to the predatory gang in power. Corruption had spread everywhere, even into the past, to taint acts that had been performed honestly.

Finally, after 10:00 A.M., the president, Cato Valandra, walked into the office, dressed as if he were on his way to church. On our poor reservation everyone, officers and tribe members alike, wore jeans and a clean shirt. But Valandra had on a suit, tie, white shirt, cuff links. If he had remembered to polish his shoes he would have looked like the "big man" he evidently considered himself to be.

He smiled when he saw me, the smile of the hawk for the sparrow. We shook hands, then I went to the window and looked out, so that he wouldn't see the disgust on my face. We discussed the "state jurisdiction" referendum, an issue we publicly agreed upon. After a few minutes he asked me if I had come back to join him. I replied that I had stopped on my way to Washington to find out how he was doing on the jurisdiction problem. To this he said bluntly, "I want to know soon if you are going to join me. I know you're planning on resigning at the NCAI convention and I don't want to see you left without anything after all the work you have done."

I told him I had to be in Washington the following evening and would give him my answer before the 4th of July.

I left Rosebud to visit my mother and father in White River, about thirty miles away. Back in my home town the people on the street swarmed around me, telling of how they were bilked of their property and how they were made to take less than the current value ($3.20) for the TLE certificates. It seemed to me the vampires in office were draining their victims without regard to how much blood they could afford to lose. As I was on the road back to the nation's capital, I realized that I had not asked about the Blue Thunder land transaction, the one mentioned by Graham Holmes.

During the next few weeks I prepared to turn over the management of the NCAI to whomever was chosen by the executive council after the upcoming convention. Then I returned to Rosebud, ready to relinquish my NCAI duties and begin the fight against the corrupt administration of my tribe.

My first step was to go directly to Cato Valandra and urge him to resign. He refused, and chose to take my request as a joke. I was never more serious in my life, and when he realized it, he knew the battle had begun. I left angrily and drove directly to the Rosebud Tribal Ranch, of which I was still president. I told the wife of the ranch manager I wanted to see the books. I gave special attention to names and the amounts of checks issued since I left the reservation in 1961. I had almost completed my review of the books when the manager appeared in the distance. I walked toward the barn to meet him, and asked about the liquor bottles and beer cans and bottles that littered the yard. He just said, "I try to keep these guys from drinking, but you know how hard it is to keep men." I stepped over to a battered pickup truck near the barn, opened the door, and found a drunken, bearded man lying on the seat. Beer cans were strewn over the floor of the truck. The stench of stale beer and liquor was everywhere. I told the manager I was requesting his resignation that day. He hemmed and hawed, telling me that we should all meet in Valentine, Nebraska, and talk things over. I left the ranch in utter disgust and returned to Rosebud.

The council office was buzzing with news of my arrival in Rosebud. A number of people I had not seen in years appeared at the office. I saw Spotted Tail and Paul Cloudman, and asked them what they knew about Julia Blue Thunder. They told me that it was not Julia Blue Thunder, but Julia Blue Horse who was involved in the land deal. I went outside, to go to my car, when a woman called my name. It was Julia Stoneman Blue Horse, a full-blooded Indian lady I had known for many years. She told me the facts of the transfer to Vetal Valandra, a BIA policeman, of her 320 acres of land that had been assigned to her for life by the tribe. Vetal Valandra had gotten her drunk, and asked for her land. Since BIA employees cannot "trade" with Indians, Valandra wanted the deal to appear as a gift from the woman to a relative, himself. It was described this way in the papers authorizing the transfer.

Schunk had signed the papers against the wall of the TLE office, without asking a question. Valandra had promised her $2,800 for signing the papers, but he withheld $800, saying he would pay her later. She tearfully asked me if I could help her recover the land. I said that I would. Then she told me that Valandra had arrested and beaten her, and warned her that he would do the same each time he saw her. He reminded her that he was backed by his cousin, Cato Valandra, and by Harold Schunk. She was plainly frightened. I assured her that she could not be arrested if she had done nothing wrong. Then I went to see her son, Antoine LaDeaux, and asked him to watch out for his mother.

On June 22, 1964, I wrote two separate letters to the Secretary of the Interior, Stewart L. Udall, in which I described the numerous situations on the reservation that indicated the corruption that existed in both the tribal and federal offices. I expected immediate action from the investigative staff of the interior department, but it wasn't until the middle of July that an investigator finally arrived.

On the 4th of July I attended a gathering in the Spring Creek community, and was invited to speak about tribal affairs. The whole Valandra family was present. After the day's ceremonies, Frank Picket Pin, the announcer, introduced me.

"My friends and relatives," I said, "I shake hands with you with a happy heart, but I only wish that all was happiness instead of the way we all know things are going in our tribal government. On July 1, 1964, Cato Valandra and [his father] Thomas Valandra,

93

Sr., filed an 'Order to Show Cause,' charging that I had made false and defamatory statements against them.* It is a near impossibility to make slanderous statements about these men. My people, remember 1950 and 1951 when Thomas Valandra was in the hay scandal, when he wiped out Indian loan clients? No, my people, you are the witnesses to these statements and I dare these men to go to any court where we can prove what I have said about them publicly. But the two Valandras have chosen to go to state court, a court that has no jurisdiction over these Indian matters. You all know how these men are beating you people on TLE certificates. Where is all the $350,000 of TLE income going to? Where is all the tribal cattle? You and I know, and I for one will fight until these men who are responsible for these acts are caught and prosecuted. I will never rest until our government does its duty and protects its words. Now the Valandras have hundreds of witnesses, so let them go to court and we shall see who is violating the law. Enjoy yourselves, my people, and hold forever unto your beautiful culture. We are rich while the materially rich are in reality poorest."

The speech was, in effect, my opening public salvo against the administration. People applauded and blared car horns in response.

While all this was taking place, I knew that my brother, a councilman from the Swift Bear community, was planning to enroll in a mechanics' training school in California, and would be resigning from his office. At the meeting held for the purpose of filling the vacancy I was nominated and elected to the councilman's post. The community officers prepared the documents attesting to my election, and submitted them to the tribal council for final approval.

Now I was charged with the legal responsibility of protecting the tribe, and I began circulating a petition among the councilmen that would demand a special council meeting to hear charges against the president of the tribe. Two-thirds of the councilmen signed the petition, the proportion required by the tribal constitution, and it was filed with the tribal secretary, along with a request that notice

* The two Valandras had filed a $200,000 slander suit in the state court in Mellette County. I knew very well they would not dare go to trial, for they were as guilty as could be of the charges I had leveled against them.

be given to all councilmen to attend a special meeting on July 8, 1964.

On that day a quorum made an appearance but no meeting was held, as the president and his cronies maneuvered to avoid the consequences of a hearing on their administration. But the next day the councilmen gathered again, and tension mounted. Suddenly a council meeting was convened, and I handed typed copies of the official charges I had made against the president to all the councilmen. I waited to be officially seated as a councilman from the Swift Bear community.

My brother's resignation was read and accepted. The tribal president, Cato Valandra, stood and asked the council not to seat me because I had not lived on the reservation for over a year. The tribal constitution calls for legal residency of a year as a requirement for tribal officials, but that was no problem since I maintained my residence in the Swift Bear community while working in Washington. I was not yet officially a councilman, and therefore was not allowed to ask for the platform to defend myself. However, I made an attempt to speak from where I was sitting, so that the tribe would know that unfair advantage was being taken by the president—who had been officially served with a notice calling for his removal.

To my amazement, the councilmen just sat, hanging their heads. In the crowd were several non-Indians with a vested interest in the tribe; I especially noticed Richard Davenport, owner of the Nebraska State Bank of Valentine, Nebraska, who held a $50,000 mortgage (illegal) on 570 head of tribal cattle, five separate notes totaling $60,000, and several thousand dollars' worth of letters of guarantee from the tribe.

Finally, Councilman Robert Moran requested that I be given the floor to state my position. President Valandra said I could, if I restricted my speech to matters regarding my council seat.

I took the floor and said that I had worked for all Indians in Washington, but that I had maintained my legal residence in South Dakota during that time, and that I was entitled to be seated as councilman.

The council voted. Nine voted against seating me, and twelve abstained from voting. I was shocked. I did not know what pressures the councilmen were under, but that they were not free to vote as they wished was clear. I had to find out why.

The president recessed the meeting without a mention of the charges against him. He thought he had, I am sure, won round two. Outside, I announced that the people would have a meeting in Clark Hall, which was down the street. In minutes the meeting was underway before a large crowd, many of whom had to stand. I was mad, and showed it as I told the crowd of the mortgage against our cattle; I showed them a certified copy of the mortgage, explaining what it meant. I told them that there was no council authority for the hundreds of guaranteed debts issued by the tribe, and that the tribal charter prohibited such activity. I explained how the administration was purchasing TLE certificates for half their value and then cashing them in for full value. I told the audience that my clash with Valandra and his cohorts was not a fight for power, but a battle for justice and for personal rights. The people stayed to shake my hand as I came down from the platform to go to my car.

A few days later, Ivan Kestner, special agent from the department of the interior, checked into the Maverick Motel in Mission, South Dakota. I helped with his investigation by bringing him to the Nebraska State Bank in Valentine to interview Richard Davenport. Davenport, I observed, was perspiring freely, although the air-conditioners were whirring away. Davenport showed us the three accounts of the tribe. The ledgers of all three were covered with entries in red ink, and he explained that the tribe had been bouncing checks for some time. The tribe had been allowed to borrow over $110,000 since February 1964, $60,000 of the amount as recently as three months before. Davenport indignantly told us that the tribe had borrowed all that money from his bank and then had the nerve to withdraw $12,000 and transfer it to the Northwest National Bank in Gregory, South Dakota. We left and had gone about a block when Kestner told me he was going back to the bank to get copies of the tribal accounts. "There seems to be something radically wrong with that bank setup," he said.

Later that day Kestner advised me that his report would support the charges I had made in my letter to the department of the interior. He continued his investigation for three days, and I was convinced that the evidence he gathered would indicate the need for a full-scale investigation. Before he left Kestner remarked that he had enough information to keep six men busy for a long time.

The rest of my stay at Rosebud before returning again to Washington was spent gathering as much evidence as I could. People sought me out and gave me details of how they were given purchase orders made out to various banks, auto agencies, grocery and clothing stores, for the sale of their land. Stanley Hatten, a fifty-year-old Indian man, told me how he had borrowed five hundred dollars from the Nebraska State Bank and repaid it to the tribal treasurer, William LaPointe, only to receive a notice from the bank of the past due note for five hundred dollars plus interest. Not only was the money not repaid to the bank by the tribe, but Hatten had never made any kind of interest agreement. Everywhere I turned Indians reported that they were unable to obtain cash for the sale of their land to the tribe, but were instead given purchase orders for merchandise that they wished to have. To top it all off, the tribal officials were retaining title to the vehicles exchanged for the purchase orders. For the time being I had to let the matter drop and return to Washington to finish up my work for the NCAI.

The NCAI Convention was held on July 28, 1964, in Sheridan, Wyoming, and on that day I officially resigned from the organization. I spoke harshly to the leaders from various tribes, who wanted the benefits of having a national organization but did not want to support it. (At this time, I was owed around $13,000* in back salary and expenses by the NCAI, a fact which provides an indication of the organization's financial status.) I charged the delegates with

* On October 8, 1964, I attended a meeting of the executive council in Denver for the purpose of meeting with a special finance committee, which was reviewing the expenditures of the NCAI from 1951 through 1964. I must have made some enemies, for Walter Wetzel advised me that a rumor was current that I had embezzled money from the NCAI. I welcomed the investigation, for it would reveal the fact that $13,048 in back salary was owed me. The executive council members decided not to carry on the review, which disappointed me. At this writing, I still have not received any part of the money due me.

97

neglecting their representative body, thereby diminishing the opportunities that an organization such as ours, based in the city where
the laws are made, could create for all Indians.

I started home from the convention. The NCAI had, I thought,
made real progress for the Indian, despite the lack of financial support. But despite any progress, I left the NCAI much as I found it
in one respect. On paper it had the potential to do infinite good for
the Indian; but that all-important ingredient, money, was missing,
and in actuality it was as weak as the paper on which its charter
was printed.

6
How to Scalp a Reservation

I returned home to the town of White River, and made arrangements to buy a house. Although the job of scraping away the corruption that enmired the tribe appeared to be enormous, I was happy to be back. My children had the fields to run in and the streams to swim in and untrafficked roads on which to ride their bikes. The whirl of Washington life, which I disliked, was immediately forgotten.

I began to collect additional reports of fraud and abuse. Silas Black Dog provided me with the first substantial case. He told me that he had repeatedly tried to sell his Tribal Land Enterprise certificates, without success. A TLE employee, Wilbur Blacksmith, had approached him and offered him a proposition: the sale of the certificates would be approved if Black Dog would kick back three hundred of the thousand dollars worth of certificates he wished to sell. Black Dog agreed, the sale was approved, and the payoff was made to the employee. Later, Black Dog brought his brother-in-law, Two Hawk, to the TLE employee. Two Hawk wanted to sell eight hundred dollars' worth of the certificates. The employee agreed to obtain approval of the sale if Two Hawk bought a car, a 1951 Ford, from him. The deal was made, and the two men began driving home to the Lower Brule Reservation from the TLE agency office at Rosebud. They had gone part of the way when the piston rod broke, damaging the engine. The car was sold for scrap metal.

Another case came to my attention shortly after the Black Dog incidents. A man, a non-Indian named Virgil Barron, who is married to an Indian, bought some hogs, and was going to use the money from his TLE certificates to pay for them. But when he went to the tribal office, as directed, he was told that the Tribal Land Enterprise was without funds. He left thinking that he would have to return the hogs. As he was walking to the car, the president's father, Tom Valandra, called him over and asked if he wanted to receive cash for his TLE Certificates. He then told the man that the sale of the Certificates could be arranged for three hundred dollars. The next day the man and his wife turned in the TLE certificates and were issued a United States Government check for $1,500. The elder Valandra accompanied the couple to the store in Rosebud, the check was cashed, and the man handed over three hundred dollars.

I reported these cases and others to the department of the interior and to Harold Doyle, the United States Attorney in Sioux Falls, but no action was taken on them. The BIA supposedly sets the value of the TLE certificates, regulates their sale, and oversees all transactions.

Throughout the remainder of that year and into 1965 I gathered evidence of corruption on the reservation, and poured reports into both federal and state offices.

I pursued the Blue Horse land case, and on May 21, 1965, the deputy commissioner of the BIA rescinded the transaction and restored the land to Mrs. Blue Horse, on the grounds that Vetal Valandra had misrepresented himself. (The case was not resolved, however, as we shall see.) But no charges stemming from Vetal Valandra's actions were placed.

The Blue Horse case was not simply a clearcut example of the kind of land thievery that took place on our reservation; all of its ramifications, and the blatant disregard of law and decency by the culprits, indicated how deep and all-encompassing the corruption had become. Mrs. Blue Horse's son, Antoine LaDeaux, had witnessed the land transaction between his mother and Vetal Valandra. Soon afterward, he was hired by the superintendent, Schunk, and placed on the payroll of the road department of Rosebud. Then, a short time later, he received over $8,000 as compensation for land that was to be preempted by the U.S. Corps of Engineers, who were constructing a large dam on the Missouri River. LaDeaux wished to buy a house, one large enough for his family of thirteen

100

children, but the Superintendent refused to approve LaDeaux's choice. A woman related to the superintendent had a house for sale, and was asking an outrageously high price of $4,000. LaDeaux was informed that the sale of this house to him had been approved, and the superintendent promptly paid the $4,000 to the woman from LaDeaux's agency account. Later, when LaDeaux wanted to sell the house and go to Texas to train as a welder, he was not permitted by the BIA to sell the house for less than he had paid for it. Three years later, however, he finally was allowed to sell—for $350. The superintendent giveth and the superintendent taketh away.

Several months after the BIA had decided to rescind the Blue Horse deal, in October 1965, I tried to obtain federal help in my fight to be seated in the tribal council. I was familiar with the Civil Rights Act of 1964, and it had occurred to me that I might be able to obtain justice under that statute. I wrote to the U.S. Attorney General on October 7, and received a reply the following week. Arthur Caldwell, an attorney in the United States department of justice, had this to tell me: "We are sorry to inform you that the Civil Rights Act of 1964 is not applicable to your case. Since the action about which you complain is action taken by an Indian tribe on the reservation, the Department of Justice has no authority to be of any assistance to you in this matter."

The Act states, "The Acts shall apply to all persons regardless of race, color, creed, religion or national origin," so it seemed I was being told that I had no race, creed, color, religion, or national origin. If it were indeed true that the federal authorities considered the Indian beyond its legal comprehension, he would probably be better off; but nearly three thousand laws and regulations and a Bureau of Indian Affairs have the Indian firmly pressed beneath the government's legal thumb.

Our frustration increased as we accumulated evidence that our tribal members were being defrauded of their money and land by the tribal administration, without local BIA intervention. I continued to send the evidence to the department of the interior, but I knew that a government agency was not likely to carry on an investigation that would reveal itself as guilty of corruption. An advisor to the Senate Indian Affairs Committee told us frankly that no senator would instigate a senate inquiry into our charges because Indians did not have enough votes to count.

Along with a few others of the tribe, I kept unearthing evidence —witnesses, documents, reports—that we hoped would some day topple the guilty tribal leaders and shake up the BIA. On August 25, 1965, I obtained through the efforts of two white men four canceled checks from Roy Hight of White River, South Dakota. Three of the checks, in amounts of $1125, $1000, and $450, were made out to the Rosebud Tribal Ranch, and one, for $740, was made out to Cal (Calvin) Valandra. The checks were payment for grazing rights on the tribal ranch. One, the check made out personally to Cal Valandra, was incontrovertible evidence that payment which should have gone to the tribal funds was being diverted into this Valandra's pocket. I gave copies of the canceled checks to the state's attorney in Winner, South Dakota, who showed them to an FBI agent. I also submitted copies of the checks to United States Attorney Doyle, accompanied by an affidavit reporting how the checks were obtained and Hight's statement describing what the payments were for. No action from either legal agency was taken.

At this time the department of the interior was investigating my charges of corruption within the department, and federal employees who supplied me with information were changing their stories when questioned by the department, for fear of losing their jobs. The department, which was of course charged with the responsibility of protecting Indian interests, was deliberately failing in that responsibility, and instead did everything in its power both to ignore the situation on the reservation and to convince itself that it was properly doing its job. I received a letter from the department of the interior (April 6, 1966) which stated that the tribal officials had executed a $45,000 mortgage on 670 head of tribal cattle without either council or BIA approval. Thus the department of the interior was admitting that the mortgage had been illegally obtained. But the other fact of $60,000 worth of bank notes illegally executed at the bank during the same period was never mentioned. The department of the interior, in admitting that the former mortgage was unauthorized, said only that the tribe had been reminded by interior officials that they were proceeding without authority. Then to crown this masterpiece of ignorance and indifference, the department went on to mention that the tribal officials were "dangerously overextending the tribes' financial position" by issuing $80,000 worth of debts of guarantee,* and admitted that such guarantees had been obtained by "pending land purchases." Not only were tribal and federal laws flagrantly violated by the mortgages and the debts of guarantee, and ignored by the very agency that was supposed to supervise such transactions, but the department's indifference to these violations cleared the way for a new class of violations, those against the Indian Allotment Acts, which provide that "said lands shall be delivered free and clear of all liens and encumbrances whatsoever to the Indian Allotee." Our land now had $80,000 worth of liens and encumbrances. The tribal officials had been allowed by the department of the interior to illegally indebt the tribe as a whole.

I can only speculate as to why a powerful agency like the department of the interior would permit violations of law to occur under its nose. My conclusion was that corruption was being covered up to prevent the exposure of incompetence within the department. Subject to political pressures from local congressmen, and to influence by powerful tribal leaders, the department had abdicated its responsibilities so thoroughly that it could not afford to investigate allegations of corruption without revealing its own part in the criminal extortion of land and money from a whole reservation. I did know that the agency superintendent kept a list of those whom he considered troublemakers. One woman, whose child had died, asked for her own money so that she could bury the child. The superintendent refused her the money, because she had marched in a demonstration against tribal and agency

---

* In a meeting at St. Frances, the new tribal treasurer, Emil Red Fish, announced that there were still $700,000 worth of guaranteed letters outstanding as of May 1, 1970.

103

officials. Thus, the victims of the powerful combination of corrupt tribal leaders and an indifferent Bureau of Indian Affairs were silenced.

The Blue Horse case continued, a prime example of the helplessness of an Indian at the hands of lawless tribal officials and lumbering bureaucrats. On June 2, 1966, the Assistant Secretary of the Interior, Harry Anderson, issued the second decision of the department, affirming the earlier decision that the land was sold in violation of federal statutes, and that the transaction was to be considered null and void. Immediately Agency Superintendent Schunk wrote Mrs. Blue Horse saying that the Tribal President Cato Valandra objected to the decision. Her land was not returned to her, nor was income from her lands given to her. Valandra took the offensive and attempted to bribe Mrs. Blue Horse into making a statement that I was coercing her into protesting the land sale. I was served with a summons to the tribal court, which was to decide whether or not I would be disbarred as a tribal attorney (I defended Indians who had no legal counsel, although I had no law degree, because the tribal court allowed laymen to qualify as tribal attorneys). I appeared before the court, without a notion of what the charges were against me. The officials hoped that Mrs. Blue Horse would testify against me, but when I called her to the stand she told how the tribal president had offered $250 if she would sign a complaint against me. The president's secretary had prepared a statement, which Mrs. Blue Horse admitted she signed, and it was then notarized by the tribal treasurer. She went on to testify that she was to receive the $250 and leave the state; when she had settled in Nebraska, she would receive more money. The agency superintendent, Schunk, gave her a check—not for $250, but for $100—and it was written against her own Agency Individual Indian Monies Account, from which she received fifty dollars each month.

The judge called Cato Valandra to the stand, and he denied her testimony and claimed that she came to him to ask that he stop me from bothering her, and that he prepared the notarized statement at her request.

I asked the court to call Agency Superintendent Schunk to the stand, only to be told that he had left town and was unavailable to testify.

The charges against me were dismissed, but the court never tried to investigate the matter of the check issued by the superintendent, and, although I specifically requested it, they never provided me with a transcript of the trial.

Not long after the trial, the South Dakota press carried a story that I was being investigated for embezzlement. A few days after the newspaper reports appeared, a pair of FBI men came to me and said they were investigating a charge that I had accepted tribal funds at the same time I had been receiving a salary from the NCAI. I told them that the president, Cato Valandra, who had been a councilman then, had proposed that the remainder of my salary due as president of the tribe be advanced to me at the time I had been elected executive director of the NCAI. The motion had carried, and my salary had been advanced to me. I knew this was another attempt to scare me, a clumsy one undoubtedly, but the men I was fighting against were hard at work to find some method of silencing me.

I had hired an able lawyer to advise me and present to the authorities the evidence I was acquiring. John Goodrich, the lawyer, was a tough, incorruptible man, and invaluable in my battle to free my reservation from the men who were destroying it. We decided that we would go to the federal court with four cases, invoking an old law that forbids any person employed in Indian Affairs from trading with the Indians, except on behalf of the United States. Goodrich consulted with Blaine Simons, one of the most outstanding lawyers in South Dakota. In August 1966 we filed four civil actions in federal court at Sioux Falls, South Dakota. We had included the Blue Horse case, for it documented precisely the crimes that were cruelest and most blatant on the reservation.

We withstood the first assault on our actions by the U.S. Attorney, who was representing the agency superintendent and by the lawyer defending Vetal and Cato Valandra.

During the months that followed, as the cases dragged through the courts, I noticed a change of tactics on the parts of the tribal officials and the BIA. Instead of issuing letters of guarantee to tribal members who sold their land to the tribe, now the tribal officials were issuing a general letter describing the sale, and directing the seller to chosen merchants, car-dealers, and banks. However, this change in form was not a change in the illegality of this form of "payment"; the council was never asked to vote on this variation of the policy of not giving an Indian seller of land the cash to which he was entitled, for that would have required, by law, the approval of the Secretary of the Interior, and would have placed responsibility directly upon the BIA. Therefore, as before, federal statutes were deliberately broken by the wheeling and dealing leaders of our tribe.

They began to cover their tracks by hiring large numbers of men and women, to be paid with federal funds received from the "War Against Poverty." In this way they reduced quickly the number of potential discontents in the tribe. In a short time almost 750 tribal members were selected to work for Office of Economic Opportunity programs. The facade had changed, but the dirty work going on behind, had not. The officers managed to find jobs within OEO programs regardless of qualifications. Sonny Waln, Jr., a man who had not even completed high school, was made director of the Rosebud Sioux's OEO programs. Waln is a relative of the tribal treasurer. Other relatives and friends of those in power were hired despite their glaring lack of experience or qualifications for jobs. Others, who the leaders felt might testify about the scandals on the reservation, also were hired; their first job was to keep their mouths shut. Of course, all of these hiring procedures were carried out in defiance of express OEO regulations forbidding such practices.

The Indians who continued to criticize the BIA and the tribal leaders soon found their lease monies frozen; they also were prevented from carrying on lawful business at the tribal offices. I gathered complaint after complaint and forwarded them to the department of the interior. To show the tribespeople, who were depending upon me to work a change in the conditions on the reservation, that I meant business, I filed three civil actions in tribal court, but the judge frankly told me, "I can't go against those guys." I waited and filed three more civil actions in tribal court, getting as far as a "show cause" order from the associate judge while the chief judge was out of town at the time, but when the chief judge returned he overruled the order and killed the actions.

Reports of Indian wolves preying on Indian sheep still came regularly to my attention. One particularly galling incident involved Susie Clairmont, the mother-in-law of the Tribal Land Enterprise manager, and Albert Swift Crockery, an Indian whom the BIA considered mentally incompetent and who was therefore supposed to be under the close supervision of the BIA in all financial dealings. Crockery told me and a special agent of the department of the interior that Mrs. Clairmont informed him that he had a check for $496 from TLE, and she would take him to Valentine, Nebraska, to cash it. Mrs. Blue Horse's son, LaDeaux, drove the two to the bank. Mrs. Clairmont had Albert Swift Crockery sign the check, and then she took the cash, giving the driver $30, pocketing $400, and giving the poor man, whose money it was, $66, and telling him that he could stay at her house any time. Albert Swift Crockery was on the Welfare Division's list of people for whom special budgetary provisions were made. Under no circumstances was he allowed to dispose of his land without the approval of the BIA superintendent.

These and other cases clearly warranted prosecution, but the authorities chose not to do a thing. All complaints seemed to be effectively blocked no matter to which agency or to which official they were referred. It was hard to believe that the men occupying the top jobs in the state and federal agencies of justice and Indian Affairs knew that corruption flourished so flagrantly in their offices, but time and time again they would not institute the investigative procedures which would have exposed the abuses taking place on the reservation.

In January 1967 Blaine Simons, one of the lawyers working on the Blue Horse case, received a letter from the interior department directing all parties to submit final arguments. Simons, Goodrich, and I prepared to present Mrs. Blue Horse's case once again. On the day of the hearing, I drove Mrs. Blue Horse, her husband, and her son and daughter-in-law to Murdo, South Dakota, where the final transcript of the facts of the case was completed. Copies of this transcript were sent to the Secretary of the Interior, the tribal attorney, the lawyer representing Vetal Valandra, the BIA police-man who had illegally obtained the land from Mrs. Blue Horse. We received copies of the information submitted by Valandra's attorney and the tribal attorney. Valandra admitted that he paid Mrs. Blue Horse $2800 for the land. His canceled check was submitted as evidence, and his attorney said that he could prove that Mrs. Blue Horse received the full $2800. On the canceled check was a legal description of the land involved, and the assignment number: A–1385.

The tribal attorney decided to be dramatic and, on behalf of the tribe, stated that if our case was upheld, the United States should prosecute those who violated the law.

After studying Valandra's version of the case, Goodrich wrote an addendum to the Blue Horse appeal. In it he pointed out that Vetal Valandra was now trying to prove that he purchased land from Mrs. Blue Horse, whereas his original story was that the land was given as a *gift* to him. This reversal of testimony, the addendum pointed out, amounted to proof of his guilt. The addendum was sent to the department of the interior. We waited for the decision.

Elections were fast approaching, and the subject of everyone's conversation on the reservation. Those in power were wielding it, reminding over seven hundred tribesmembers that they owed their jobs to the present administration. I ran again for council president, and was defeated by forty votes. However, my loss was engineered by denying the vote to the people who resided in the reservation towns of Winner, Colome, Dallas, Gregory, Burke, Herrick, and St. Charles. These were towns which had voted for me in the primary elections.

The Valandras were on the move that summer of 1967. The BIA—and Vetal Valandra—reached a new low when Valandra, with the approval of the BIA, cut and harvested 7169 bales of hay from the Blue Horse land, which had been ordered restored

108

to Mrs. Blue Horse and was now under appeal to the department of the interior. Mrs. Blue Horse filed charges against Vetal Valandra in tribal court, only to have her complaint ignored completely. She, her husband, and I went out to her property to see if we could stop the hay harvesting; only a young workman was there and he left after we read him the secretary of interior's letter declaring the transaction null and void.

The following morning the trucks were back. The workers told us that the agency superintendent and the tribal officers had given them permission to proceed with haying. It was evident that the men who had perpetrated the swindle were not content with twisting the law to their own ends, but felt that they were beyond the law.

We raced to Murdo, to have Goodrich call the Secretary of the Interior in a desperate effort to stymie the agency authorities. We were told, as usual, that the matter would be looked into. Goodrich wrote to members of the United States Senate, only to receive the same response. It appeared as if nothing could be done to prevent someone from openly and brazenly robbing an Indian.

Suddenly, eleven days after the tribal elections, November 6, 1967, the Assistant Secretary of the Interior, Harry Anderson, rendered a final decision on the Blue Horse land case. The decision upheld Mrs. Blue Horse and made these points:

> . . . [Mrs. Blue Horse] relinquished her land assignment of 320 acres to the Rosebud Sioux Tribal Land Enterprise (TLE) upon condition that it be reassigned to Mr. Vetal Valandra as a gift. Representation was made that (Mrs. Blue Horse) was the aunt of Mr. Valandra, although in fact they are not related.
>
> The object of misrepresenting the transaction as a gift from aunt to nephew was apparently to evade the provisions of Federal law prohibiting Indian employees of the United States from trading with Indians, without Secretarial approval.
>
> Although the Superintendent purportedly approved the transfers, he was not authorized to do so.
>
> According to the bylaws of the TLE, the value of interests should be revised annually to conform to current land values.

109

In 1958 the value of an interest was fixed at $2.98. This was increased to $3.30 in July 1962. The August 1966 value was $3.60 per interest. Nevertheless $2.98 per interest was used as the basis for compensating [Mrs. Blue Horse] for her 781 interests in 1963, although it should have been at least $3.30. This was in violation of bylaw 26 of the TLE. . . . Moreover, the land was leased for a five-year term beginning March 1, 1962, at a rental of $482.50 a year—more than one-sixth of the price paid by Mr. Valandra. This proportionately high rental income in itself indicates that the land was obtained by Mr. Valandra for much less than its value. . . .

It is reported that in July 1967 [Valandra] harvested 120 tons of hay, valued at $20 a ton, from the land, which is apparently not now under lease. The fact that agency officers apparently permitted [Valandra] to crop the land and retain the proceeds, notwithstanding they had been instructed to impound and hold the rents in previous years when the land had been under lease, is not explained. But the value of the crop further evidences that the consideration paid [Mrs. Blue Horse] was unconscionably inadequate.

The transaction between [Mrs. Blue Horse] and Mr. Valandra was, therefore, not only not approved—because the Superintendent lacked such authority—but unapprovable, and Mr. Valandra's conduct was in violation of the Federal laws referred to above.

Equity demands, moreover, not only that the land be restored to [Mrs. Blue Horse], but that the income accruing from the lands since April 5, 1963—i.e., the rents received by Mr. Valandra in 1964, the value of the hay harvested in 1967, and the rents for 1965 and 1966 now held in escrow—also be paid to her.

Anderson went on to rule that the TLE was a party to a fraudulent and inequitable transaction, and instructed the TLE to return the land to Mrs. Blue Horse and to credit her account with the rental income for 1965 and 1966. Valandra was told to return the rental income he received in 1964 from the land and to account to Mrs. Blue Horse for the hay harvested in 1967.

I expected that the next step would be the prosecution of

criminals. I couldn't have been more mistaken. Despite the definitive statement of the department of the interior that violations of law had taken place, no indictments were forthcoming. The FBI investigated the case, and a federal grand jury had "no-billed" their inquiry into it. Not even a slap on the wrist for the perpetrators of a premeditated, vicious swindle of one of their own people. Perhaps we were expected to be so happy at having been told by the Great White Father that we were in the right, that we would forget about the wrongdoers.

Finally, on the days of November 18, 19, 25, and 26, 1968, more than a year after the Blue Horse case had been brought to the attention of the authorities, we went to trial before District Judge Fred Nickels, in Pierre, South Dakota. The judge heard the four pending civil actions which were entitled "United States, ex rel Robert Burnette, vs. Vetal Valandra, Harold Schunk, and Cato Valandra." I had to bring the suits under a federal statute which allowed an Indian to use the name of the United States. My suit was made in the only manner possible—not as a charge of fraud or theft or swindle, but under the law that said: "No person employed in Indian Affairs shall have any interest or concern in any trade with Indians, except for, and on account of, the United States; and any person offending herein, shall be liable to a penalty of $5000 and shall be removed from his office." Despite the evidence and the decision of the Secretary of the Interior on November 6, 1967, Federal Judge Fred Nickels, dismissed the four cases without taking note of the law involved. In a judgment delivered early in 1969, Judge Nickels dismissed the case on the grounds that it was a simple matter of one Indian doing business with another Indian, which is allowable within the federal statutes. I cannot help feeling his action was also an expression of disdain for me and my attorney, John Goodrich.

The Blue Horse case is a prime example of the reservation Indian's vulnerability to wolves, whether dressed in white's or Indian's clothing. The lessons of the case are clear to me; one, that the BIA is a hopeless bureaucracy that cares little for the people in its charge; two, that the United States government will tread lightly when their own employees are proven criminals; and three, that to save himself the Indian must resist assimilation into despicable customs of white wheeler-dealer, politico types. Schunk and the Valandras are the most white-assimilated, Indian-traitor Sioux I know.

Here again was another lesson on "American Justice," for we had without doubt shown that federal laws were violated, and the witnesses for the defendants admitted that the transaction began as a gift and that the relationship between Vetal Valandra and Mrs. Blue Horse was nonexistent. The Secretary of the Interior had ruled that the case was one where misrepresentations were made to circumvent the law, and still the federal judge ruled in favor of those who violated federal laws.

We are not deterred by this ruling, and we will press on with our knowledge that right is right, even when the crime is committed by a federal official. We are appealing our case to a higher court in an effort to find that elusive American dream of "Justice." And we shall find it one day soon. Until then, we Indians will pursue our goal with greater vigor and persistence, for we believe that somewhere, someplace there are truly honest men who will champion our cause, as here in America there are millions of good people who will not stand idly by while Indians are being swindled. To this end we will dedicate our lives.

7
Death
and Non-Taxes

During the late Spring of 1966, while I was embroiled in the Blue Horse case, a number of other significant incidents occurred. First were a couple of elections, as rotten as could be imagined, which I will describe in the next chapter. The second was the tragic death of Norma Jean Le Roy. It seemed to me that suddenly all the possible ills that could afflict a reservation were raging in Rosebud. Each incident led back in time to other incidents of exploitation, incompetence, and carelessness, and forward smack into the mountainous obstacles to justice presented by tribal corruption, BIA callousness, and state and federal indifference. The situation of the reservation Indian, and of the Rosebud Sioux especially, was a nightmare. His life was always and inescapably being stained by tribal corruption, white exploitation, BIA bungling, and the fantastic legal confusion that governed the relationship between the tribe and federal authorities. The poor, uneducated Indian—too poor to offer a bribe, too weak to steal—was truly without rights, and prey to anything a little bigger, a little richer, a little nastier, that crossed his path. I was to become almost overwhelmed by the events that occurred and were occurring during that spring and summer of 1966, for they were to lead me into just about every rotten dark corner of reservation Indian life. The simplest step toward justice, taken each day a thousand times by thousands of white Americans, was to be for us years of travel.

On June 4, 1966, at evening, Norma Jean Le Roy, mother of five children, walked out of the town of Mission, South Dakota, toward her home. LeRoy Sitting Bear, driving in the same direction, stopped and asked her if she would like a lift. As Norma Jean Le Roy was stepping into Sitting Bear's car, another auto, driven by Victor Left Hand Bull, crashed into the rear of the

113

Sitting Bear car. The woman was thrown into a ditch and yelled to Sitting Bear to go get the police. As Sitting Bear ran to the Maverick Hotel looking for help, he saw a third car, lights out, speed toward the two wrecked cars. The third car, driven by Louise Kelly Piocotte, turned sharply to miss the stationary cars, struck the outside fender of Left Hand Bull's car, and skidded sideways over the body of Norma Jean Le Roy.

The city police arrived minutes later, but Norma Jean Le Roy was dead, pinned beneath the third car, which turned out to be owned by Dana Farmer of St. Francis, South Dakota. Several witnesses reported that all nine occupants of the two cars that had crashed into Sitting Bear's car fled the scene of the accident.

After twenty minutes or so the state police arrived and began measuring distances, questioning witnesses, and untangling the smashed cars. The city police rounded up the people who had run away, including Left Hand Bull, and turned them over to the Rosebud authorities. The personal belongings of Norma Jean Le Roy were turned over to the same authorities. I learned later that included in her effects were two sealed envelopes she had intended to give to me and Aaron De Sersa, who also was fighting the corruption of the reservation. The envelopes contained information from the files of the Rosebud Sioux tribe offices, where Norma Jean Le Roy had worked in the office of the tribal treasurer. Also included in the information in the envelopes were facts about the police force as well as about tribal fund expenditures. The envelopes were to become the objects of a search by De Sersa and myself.

Shortly after the accident, LeRoy Sitting Bear came to me and asked me to represent him. He had been arrested and charged with culpability in the accident. I took the case, and on the day of the trial we appeared at the court in Rosebud, only to discover that all the court documents, including Sitting Bear's bond papers, had disappeared. I waited awhile, and then asked for dismissal of the case on the grounds that there were no legal charges before the court. The judge dismissed the case, and Sitting Bear received his bond refund.

At this time I began to investigate the problem of the missing

114

envelopes. I was assured by those who saw Mrs. Le Roy earlier the evening of her accident that she had had the envelopes in her purse. I contacted Mrs. Le Roy's parents, Mr. and Mrs. Rufus Eastman, and they said that they and their other daughter, Mrs. Pat Iyott, would go to the police station and claim the dead woman's belongings. They asked me if anything could be done to provide for their dead daughter's children, and I told them I would, through John Goodrich, institute a suit in the name of the children, if it was legally possible.

Several days later the Eastmans told me that at the police station, the BIA special officer, Peter Pychlynn, refused to give them the purse. I was not overly surprised, for Pychlynn, the highest-ranking officer on the reservation had had a run-in with Pat Iyott, the Eastmans' son-in-law, the previous year. The story of that run-in is interesting, and needs to be told here so that one can understand the context in which the Le Roy case proceeded.

The year before Mrs. Le Roy's fatal accident, I had conducted an investigation into the tribal police force, which was notoriously lax in the performance of its duties. The specific case which provoked this investigation, and the hearing which resulted, concerned policeman Lavern Cordry's grievances against actions of his superiors and revealed the extent of the rottenness of the police department. I represented Cordry at the United States Civil Service Hearing on December 14, 1965. Cordry's first witness, Charles Herman, a tribal policeman, testified that on the day of the annual Tribal Land Enterprise meeting the tribal superintendent ordered him to "babysit" with the tribal secretary, whom the tribal leaders did not want to appear at the meeting because he was drunk. Herman related other instances of abuse of the powers of policemen, of discrimination within the department against Iyott and Cordry. Herman's testimony concluded at noon, and after a break for lunch the hearing continued at 1:30 P.M. The hearing chairman immediately announced that Herman wished to withdraw his testimony, because the tribal president would dismiss him from his job if he didn't. I agreed to allow the testimony to be withdrawn but only on the condition that the reason for the withdrawal be entered into the trial records, which was done.

The hearing, originally scheduled for one day, extended from December 14 to December 17. Officers Frank Brave Bull and Edward Herman (no relation to Charles Herman), Pat Iyott and Vetal Valandra all testified that the police department was in turmoil, disorganized, and demoralized. They all indicated that most of a police officer's time was spent trying to catch other officers doing something wrong. Vetal Valandra admitted that he slept on duty and was aware that photographs had been taken of him while asleep. The Bureau of Indian Affairs' area office at Aberdeen, South Dakota (the office to which the Rosebud office was responsible), became concerned about the hearing and sent down their solicitor to defend the Rosebud captain and special officer, who were being tried for harassing Cordry. But the testimony against the two top brass, and against the police department in general, kept rolling in.

At one point, after we had summed up our presentation of evidence, the defense called Lloyd One Star, a former police officer, to the stand to testify that Cordry had harassed him. He accused Cordry of mocking full-blood Indians, thus causing One Star, himself a full-blood Indian, to resign from his position as a policeman. In my cross-examination I asked One Star why he was appearing. He replied, "They told me if I came here and told the truth, I would get a job." Such a statement would be ludicrous if it did not so tragically point up the casualness with which witnesses, indeed any observer, could be bought by a promise of a job or a few dollars. I let his statement echo in the hearing room, and then asked One Star if he had ever slept on duty while a policeman. He said, yes, he had, because he had been tired. What must appear as ridiculous naivete on his part is, unfortunately, the worst kind of sophistication. Sleeping policemen were the rule, not the exception, and I doubt anyone considered such an act as anything but the normal performance of duty.

After four days of the hearing, I had uncovered enough evidence to demand a major clean-up of the police force. But the BIA, protecting their own as always, stepped in. Officer Brave Bull was forced to transfer. Officer Edward Herman resigned and was relocated in California. Officer Iyott was pressed to transfer, but stood

116

firm. Eventually he was placed in the BIA Soil Conservation Department, where he worked until he won a decision to be returned to the agency police force. Officer Charles Herman, who was expecting a new job, was hired immediately by the city of Mission's police department. Officer Cordry took an examination for the postmaster's position at Rosebud, and obtained the job. The BIA had ignored the evidence and brushed all the dirt away from its view. So the following year, when we attempted to enlist the police's cooperation in the case of Norma Jean Le Roy, we expected to run into resistance.

I finally had to have the tribal judge order Officer Pychlynn to return the dead woman's purse to her mother and sister. A series of stupid remarks by the special officer about the purse revealed that he was familiar with its contents. Upon checking, we were not surprised to find that the two envelopes were missing. We would never find them, although we discovered the nature of the information from Mrs. Pat Iyott, Norma Jean's sister. There were records of misused tribal funds, and run-downs on police activities involving top BIA officials.

At this time, John Goodrich and I began to think about filing a suit in behalf of the surviving Le Roy children, in response to the Eastmans' request that I take steps to protect Mrs. Le Roy's children. The federal courts required that a jurisdictional act be cited in the complaint. The term "jurisdictional act" is used to file a federal court case because in each and every instance the person filing suit must cite a federal statute that gives his case a foundation on which to enter federal court.

In the matter of Norma Jean Le Roy, an Indian, we could find no way to secure jurisdiction on which to enter court, simply because Indians are "wards" of the United States government and therefore unable to enter court as "persons." The legal assumption is that we are under the care of the government and that the government must, or at least should, provide full protection under the law—a legal obligation which they have failed miserably to fulfill, as the records will prove on almost any reservation in the nation.

Unfortunately, every reservation has its Norma Jean Le Roys, whose deaths reek with the injustice that comes from the callous application of law enforcement procedures and pure laziness on the part of officials in charge of investigation of Indian crimes. It was during the course of my research on this case that I became convinced that reservation Indians were totally without legal status. As "wards of the United States," we were legally helpless; although I had received several letters from the White House, the justice department, the BIA, and the department of the interior telling me exactly that, somehow I had never accepted the fact that Indians were without any legal remedy. Now I was forced to face the fact. We had no means of pressing a suit for the negligent death of Norma Jean Le Roy.

We could not appeal to the laws of the state of South Dakota because Indians did not come under the jurisdiction of the state, nor could we turn to the politically controlled tribal courts—some of the people involved in the accident were relatives of tribal officials—and we could not invoke federal laws. Here was a situation where one Indian could kill another without fear of civil or criminal prosecution. We were excluded from the protection of the laws of the United States.

In my research I had come across what I thought to be the core of this cruel dilemma. In reading through the law books I found an act of April 8, 1866, entitled "Chapter XXXI—An Act to Protect All Persons in the United States in Their Civil Rights, and Furnish a Means of Their Vindication." It said, in part, "Be it enacted by the Senate and House of Representatives of the United States of America in Congress assembled, That all persons born in the United States and not subject to any foreign power, excluding Indians non-taxed, are hereby declared to be citizens of the United States. . . ." Further research led me to Article I of the Constitution, which contained the same phrase: "excluding Indians not taxed. . . ."

This phrase, I thought, was the source of Indian troubles. All the letters I had received informing me that various acts and laws did not apply in the cases I described, although they did not specify this phrase, seemed to refer to this exclusion. In a letter from Robert L. Bennett, commissioner of the Bureau of Indian Affairs, the situation is well defined: "Since you have been advised by the Civil

Rights Division of the Department of Justice that the Civil Rights Act does not apply to actions by an Indian tribe on a reservation, it would seem that you would petition the Congress to amend the Civil Rights Act."

Quite simply, reservation Indians were at the complete and utter mercy of tribal officials and BIA overlords, and though they were citizens of the United States, they had no recourse to any of the legal rights other American citizens enjoyed.

My first step in an attempt to obtain the minimal constitutional guarantees for reservation Indians was to write Senator Sam J. Ervin of North Carolina. Ervin had done worthy work in the area of Indian rights, having participated on the Senate Subcommittee on Constitutional Rights of American Indians. I wrote him my opinion about the crucial phrase, and how it precluded Indian rights; I also outlined the need for Congress to amend the laws so that we might appeal for protection to the courts of the United States. I suggested that when appropriate legislation was developed the words "including Indians not taxed" be inserted.

I heard that the statutes would be reviewed, and there was nothing more to be done on my part but to wait and see what developed in the Senate. I had, of course, been thinking of Norma Jean Le Roy and her children when I began investigating the Indian's lack of rights. It was a dramatic instance of the tragedy that could strike an Indian family, who could obtain neither compensation nor justice for their loss.

But I thought also of hundreds of lesser actions not involving loss of life, but usually land, which, had there been recourse to federal courts, could have been prevented. The following examples are representative of dealings on a reservation, and illustrate the Indian's plight at the hands of unscrupulous men who are the *law*, and cannot be brought to court to answer for their actions.

Real estate is probably the prime target of the tribal and local wheeler-dealers, and violations of justice and decency are commonplace in land dealings. I would estimate that over $30 million in income is lost each year by Indian landowners because of the failure of BIA officials to protect these people from unscrupulous dealers. During the World War II years, for example, the federal govern-

119

ment allowed Rosebud tribal members to lease their grasslands for sixteen cents an acre, while whites whose lands adjoined our reservation were leasing their lands for two dollars an acre. Our farmlands leased for one dollar and twenty-five cents an acre while white farmlands leased for more than three dollars an acre. All these leases had been approved by our "benefactors" in the BIA, who were charged with the responsibility of preventing Indians from going out and making foolish deals.

It was during these years that the Tribal Land Enterprise was devised by the BIA. Whatever its original intent, this one organization has served more efficiently to separate the Indian from his land than any other agency I know. The BIA superintendent would order all employees to transport any Indian who wished to sell his land directly to the TLE offices. Elderly Indians fell victim to promises which, of course, turned out to be false. Hundreds on our reservation presented their lands to TLE, expecting to receive large sums of money, plus a bonus from the prospective buyer of their lands, but all they received were the almost worthless TLE certificates, which eventually sold for ten cents on the dollar. I know Indians who lost 160 acres of land, and were given in compensation seventy-five dollars or a single horse. The land appraisals were another matter that stunk to high heaven. Appraisals were made from an office desk at Rosebud, by a BIA official, whose job included being familiar with current land values. At one point during the ten-year period from 1943 to 1953, Indian land was being sold at three dollars per acre while white-owned land in the nearby counties of Tripp, Mellette, Gregory, Lyman, and Todd was selling for fifteen to thirty dollars an acre. Of course, thousands of acres passed from Indian to non-Indian hands during that time—all with full approval from our federal protectors.

I had collected case after case of swindles, sharp dealings, criminality. It seemed incredible, even to an Indian who grew up on a reservation and witnessed day in and day out the mischief created by the BIA, that some of the deals they promoted could be so blatantly unjust.

A knowledgeable federal employee approved the sale of 160

acres of land for $480 in 1950. An elderly full-blood Indian woman, unable to speak or understand the English language, was advised by her son, in cahoots with a white rancher who wanted the woman's land, to sell her property to the TLE. She did so, receiving $1,920 in devalued TLE certificates for her 320 acres. (It was common knowledge that the land had a real market value of twenty dollars per acre.) The poor woman, after her son disposed of the certificates for what he could, had virtually nothing. This legalized swindle had another repulsive aspect to it, since the BIA, which had to approve the sale of the land, is supposed to take special interest in those Indians who, like this uneducated woman, are at an obvious disadvantage.

In cases where a white wanted to "trade" lands with an Indian, he would contact a man on the reservation who was known to promote such deals, and this man would influence the landowner to turn his lands into TLE. Once this was accomplished, the board of directors of TLE would take over and make the deal for the "exchange" of lands. One white rancher, who went so far as to pay a per diem to the entire tribal council, used to exchange large tracts of land with TLE. In these exchanges he usually was favored by receiving two tribal acres for every one of his, even though his land, in Mellette County, where water problems exist, was worth less than the tribal land in Todd County.

This kind of loss, giving more land than the tribe received in return, exchanging good land for bad, was common. Indian farmlands on the eastern end of the reservation received twice the rainfall of the western end of our reservation. However, the TLE was trading off lands in the eastern area to white farmers and ranchers who were giving the tribe land in the less valuable western region of this area of the reservation.

Thus, during the postwar years, the quality and quantity of our all-important land base was eroded seriously, with full BIA approval. Nor should one get the idea that such swindles ceased twenty years ago. In 1962 the BIA offices in Crow Agency, Montana, were approving leases for the grand sum of *eight cents* per acre. John Cummins, the chairman of the Crow tribe, ended this

121

scandalous practice, but no one, to my knowledge, was ever reprimanded, nor were any of the luckless Indian lessors compensated fairly.

These examples are obvious cases where the victim, had he had recourse to the courts, most likely would have found satisfaction. But the "thieves," observed by Sherman in his famous definition of an Indian reservation, operate without fear of prosecution.

I continued my research, trying to discover some regulation or precedent that would provide a foundation in court to pursue the Norma Jean Le Roy case. Without civil rights, the Indian seemed to be pointed back to the provisions of the many treaties he had signed. Yet the treaty with the Sioux Indians signed by South Dakota on April 29, 1868, provided that any offender against the Indians was to be tried under the laws of the United States. Here it seemed was a possibility, if a prosecuting attorney so wished, to attempt to obtain justice in the Norma Jean Le Roy case.

I wrote to the U.S. Attorney in Sioux Falls, South Dakota, about the death of Mrs. Le Roy. He answered me that an investigation would be made. After a period of time, when I realized that nothing was going to be done, I consulted with friends on the reservation who also were gathering evidence of corruption in tribal affairs. We discussed possible strategies by which we could galvanize the federal authorities into action, however small. We decided to invest in a trip to Washington where we would try to present the evidence we had been gathering directly to higher-rank officials in the department of the interior. Early in the month of July 1966, Henry Crow Dog and I left the Rosebud reservation on our way to the nation's capital.

In Washington, the first person we chose to see was Mr. Harry R. Anderson, Assistant Secretary of the Interior. We presented the Norma Jean Le Roy case and other examples of misconduct, specifically the records of the chattel mortgages signed by tribal officers after the tribal officials had received an order from Anderson prohibiting any further mortgages that did not fulfill the provisions of the tribal charter. The mortgages, totaling $19,735, for cattle already mortgaged for $45,000 by the now defunct Nebraska

State Bank of Valentine, disturbed Anderson, and he questioned us closely about them.

Next, we brought up the subject of the TLE. We asserted that TLE received and expended 75 percent of the tribal income—approximately $325,000 per year—on a fraudulent basis. The amount of money made and spent dubiously by the TLE could have amounted to $1,950,000 since 1960. We reviewed details of TLE land schemes, examples of individual Indians who had been defrauded by TLE in the purchase of their lands. Anderson listened, asking an occasional question. When Henry Crow Dog and I left his office, we felt that we had accomplished our mission: to expose the corruption on the Rosebud reservation to an official who had the power and the responsibility to begin measures that would rectify the situation.

My next stop was the department of justice. I had an appointment with the assistant attorney general, Edwin Weisel, Jr. I liked Weisel upon meeting him, and he seemed quite interested in Indian problems. I reviewed the Norma Jean Le Roy case, and the evidence of frauds—for example, the Blue Horse case—in which no indictments had ever been made. He listened patiently as I went into detail after detail, and showed him the documentation that we gathered in Rosebud of the variety of violations and swindles that were taking place there. I covered much ground, from evidence that an FBI agent had falsified a report on the Blue Horse land deal,* to the police role in the disappearance of the envelopes from Mrs. Le Roy's purse, and through the evidence that indicated that tribal officials were violating both federal and tribal laws. He seemed impressed by the accumulation of evidence, and told me that he would check into each case.

Nothing ever came of Norma Jean's case, but it served to put Indians on notice that they were being discriminated against by the United States government by being denied of the "due process of law" promised to all citizens by the Constitution.

* The FBI agent's report, that caused the Blue Horse case to be "no-billed" before the federal grand jury, contradicted the findings of the Secretary of the Interior in his November 6, 1967 ruling.

123

Norma Jean Le Roy's case stands as an invisible monument depicting the ugly fact that in the once-beautiful land of the American Indians, the Land of the Free and the Home of the Brave that prides itself on freedom, equality, and justice, Indians are no better off than the slaves were 150 years ago. Our lives and property in reality are so controlled that the Indian is made into a public liability, instead of being allowed to contribute to society as a whole.

Meanwhile, we Indians live in a hell created by the federal government, whose savage power exploits the once-proud Indian nations by forcing us to swallow programs that belittle us as human beings. But we Indians are as strong as water and as flexible as the winds. We shall resist oppression, and we shall survive.

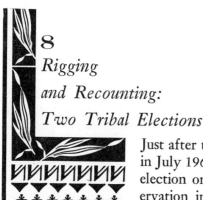

8
Rigging
and Recounting:
Two Tribal Elections

Just after the Norma Jean Le Roy tragedy, in July 1966, I became involved in the tribal election on the Cheyenne River Sioux reservation in South Dakota. I had been familiar with the maneuverings of tribal politicians who wished to retain their power, but I had not come up against such brazen election-rigging until I observed the Cheyenne River elections. The summer of the following year was to see me involved in the Rosebud elections, and undergoing almost exactly the same tactics at the hands of the Valandra gang.

The most vicious aspect of the kind of political abuse within the tribal governmental setup that I shall be reporting is that it completely stifles the reservation members. They cannot appeal beyond the council, beyond the president, if they are dissatisfied with the conditions of his local government. It is precisely at the level of the tribal officials that so many of the abuses occur, in regard to both person and property, for which the individual Indian cannot receive redress. He is powerless in the face of dictatorial tribal leaders sanctioned by the BIA, and subject to the whims of both powers. What is needed, obviously, is somebody or some agency, composed of legal and investigative people, who could be appealed to by Indians when they felt that there was abuse of the responsibilities assigned to tribal officials.

It was strange for me to witness the Cheyenne River election, and then to participate in the Rosebud elections, for it did not seem possible that what went on could be taking place in the United States in the 1960s. The rigged elections in South Vietnam had been recently exposed, and the frustration and anger that I felt toward the actions of our "leaders" were, I supposed, akin to the reactions of those in Communist and Fascist countries who are told that they have a voice in determining their own leaders, and

125

then discover that the only voice that is heard is the voice of power, and that elections have a magical way of turning out just the way the powers-that-be intended.

On a hot July afternoon in 1966 I had a visit from Ramon Williams, a Cheyenne River Sioux from Eagle Butte, South Dakota. He was running for tribal chairman in the upcoming Cheyenne River Sioux reservation elections, against the incumbent Frank Ducheneaux. He knew that I had had some fair experience in tribal politics, especially in situations that were, to say the least, unusual. Williams was well aware that the machine in power would try everything to defeat him, and he wanted my advice and assistance in his campaign.

Williams filled me in on the background to the impending elections. On May 10 the chairman of the election committee, Alex Chasing Hawk, certified the candidacy of Williams, but gave him the mandatory choice, which was unconstitutional, of resigning his post as councilman or having his name withheld from the primary election ballot. No one expected Williams to succeed in the primary, and if he chose to run chances were excellent that he would be completely out of the tribal government. Williams decided to take the chance. To the surprise of everyone who was familiar with the Cheyenne River Sioux's leaders, he scored an astounding upset victory of 299 to 112 over Frank Ducheneaux in the primary. The fat was in the fire. The Ducheneaux clan, much like the Valandras, had been in power for some time, and they were not about to relinquish it to the first person who came along and beat them in a fair election. Williams knew that.

Williams began to campaign for the tribal chairman's position, and I stayed in the background, trying to guess the opposition's tactics. The tribal council began to unpack its weapons. Their heavy artillery was financial: they dipped into tribal funds to make loans to reservation members, especially those Indians who might be tempted to vote against the Ducheneaux machine. The council controlled the Office of Economic Opportunity's "War on Poverty" program, and potential discontents were immediately placed on the program's payroll and then threatened with dismissal if they chose to continue their political activities. The wife of the owner of the

126

local county newspaper in Eagle Butte was one of the people hired for the OEO program; it was expected that the incumbent administration would receive handsome publicity in the paper.

Ramon Williams appealed directly to the Bureau of Indian Affairs, asking them to ensure that the election would be carried on honestly. He also wrote to Senator George McGovern, Chairman of the Senate's Subcommittee on Indian Affairs, telling him of his fears and asking for assurance that the elections would be properly handled. McGovern evidently asked the BIA to keep close watch over the election proceedings, and Williams was informed that all necessary steps to ensure an honest election would be taken. Williams, his fears allayed, continued with his campaign. He knew, from his primary victory, that many of the Cheyenne River Sioux were hoping that the strangle hold the Ducheneaux family had on the tribal government could be broken, and that leaders could be elected who would reverse more than a decade of corruption and impoverishment.

One of the sorest issues was the $10,600,000 Oahe Dam project that was carried out between 1954 and 1956. Before the settlement the tribal leaders had been informed that the U.S. Corps of Engineers was going to construct a dam that would flood an area in the Missouri River Valley 121 miles long, on which considerable Indian land was situated. The tribal leaders of the Cheyenne Sioux immediately began plans to purchase as much individual Indian trust land as they could that fell within the proposed dam site. A good many individual Indians who, of course, knew nothing of the planned dam, succumbed to offers by the tribal leaders. Thousands of acres were bought up by the council for as low as five dollars per acre. This newly acquired land—bought with full BIA approval and BIA knowledge of the proposed dam—was assigned by tribal council members to their relatives.

While these transactions were taking place, the council had another bright, profitable idea. The council gained the support of the department of the interior for legislation which would change the lifetime tribal assignments to land held by tribal individuals to trust titles, thus placing such land at the disposal of the tribal officials—the Council. This legislation was introduced into Congress in 1954,

127

cheerfully backed by the BIA as a means of giving individual Indians title to lands secured cheaply from the tribal program designed to consolidate the multiple-ownership lands that had developed since the Allotment Act of 1887 as individual Indians died, leaving their lands to their heirs, causing such lands to become fragmented until it was unmanageable.

Over the years, those elected tribal leaders and their relations had accumulated lifetime assignments on lands purchased by the tribe to eliminate the heirship problem. But such lands were held in trust by the United States for the Cheyenne River Sioux tribe and could not be sold or encumbered except by act of Congress. The scheme was to convince Congress to pass legislation that would give individuals trust title to lands now owned by the entire tribe, thereby creating a profit motive on the part of these lifetime assignees.

I was president of the Rosebud Sioux at the time, and was concerned to see this piece of legislation being considered in Congress. I did some checking, and to my amazement I discovered the bill had been proposed at the request of the Cheyenne River Sioux. I was bewildered—why should an Indian tribe be interested in the passage of legislation that weakened the legal bond between the individual Indian and the land he held? An unsuspecting assistant commissioner of Indian Affairs mentioned to me that the Cheyenne River Sioux were negotiating with the Army for a settlement on the lands that the dam would take.

I went over to the Cheyenne River reservation and did some asking around. I found plenty of Indians who had been enticed by ready cash into quick sales of their lands to the tribe. Life assignments to these lands were then purchased from the tribe by Council members' relatives. The proposed legislation passed into law, and trust patent titles were given to those tribal members holding tribal assignments to real estate. In this way land passed from individual Indians to the tribe and then to other private individuals—the council members and their relatives. Soon after accomplishing the accumulation of a great part of the land to be claimed by the construction of the Oahe Dam, the tribe settled with the U.S. Corps of Engineers for approximately fifty-five dollars per acre. The profit—of fifty dollars per acre in some instances—bordered on

128

criminal, and the BIA, which had been aware of the dam, the sales, and the legislation, was as guilty as the wheeler-dealer council. In fact, the BIA's approval was needed for each and every maneuver and manipulation made by the Cheyenne River Sioux council. In this way certain tribal officials and their relatives were allowed to exploit their own tribespeople; one family, it was rumored, realized a profit of over $100,000. This blatant disregard for the welfare of the tribe and the greed of the tribal leaders was very much in the minds of the Cheyenne River Sioux. The precarious balance of power held by the administration through intimidation and bribery had been tipped by Williams in the primary.

The leaders still retained considerable power, however. The council set up a program that gave themselves control over a multi-million-dollar rehabilitation program, including the right to extend loans of tens of thousands of dollars to members of the tribe. Those discontented with the administration, mostly full-blood Indians, were left out of the loan program, and consequently they objected. To still the dissenting voices, the council and the BIA adopted a program whereby all tribal members would get a small sum of money.

Ramon Williams was attacking not only a corrupt administration who knew every dirty political trick in the book, but an administration to which an enormous number of the tribal members were obligated—for jobs, for money, for favors. Frank Ducheneaux, who looked like he would be more at home in Chicago than on a reservation, was a virtual dictator in the way he ran the reservation. He had the power to force the council to seat his brother, who had been convicted of a felony, as a councilman despite the tribal constitution's specific prohibition of persons with criminal records becoming councilmen.

Ducheneaux was directly responsible for the passage of one resolution by the council that forced Williams to resign his council seat before being certified to run for tribal chairman, and for another resolution assigning the tribal councilmen to act as the tribal election committee.

With all these cards stacked against him, Williams continued his campaign against Ducheneaux, and I helped in what ways I could.

129

I wrote an open letter to Frank Ducheneaux, questioning an expenditure of $100,000 that he and other tribal leaders in the area had supported to construct a Sioux Indian Village. This project had been announced as a monument to the endurance of the Sioux. It was a $100,000 blunder. Its sponsors thought it would be a profitable tourist attraction, but the large nondescript building at Wasta, South Dakota, drew few tourists. And a scheme to profiteer off the Sioux people—their own people—backfired.

My letter got some attention, for while I attended a meeting with Williams in Eagle Butte, South Dakota, in September 1966, I was threatened with arrest by Ducheneaux's police on the charge of being an undesirable person (such a phrase exists in the federal statutes, and the charge can be made). Nevertheless, I spoke to a group of Cheyenne River Sioux at Dupree, and reviewed a claim, made by the Sioux Nation, for compensation for 72 million acres of land taken from us in defiance of the U.S. treaty with the Sioux Indians of April 29, 1868.

The claim had been pending for many years, and back in 1956 a number of us wished to replace the attorney, Ralph Case, who was handling the claim. We respected Case for his long fight for justice for the Sioux, but he was old and ill, and that year he planned legal action that would have precluded the successful appeal of claim. Frank Ducheneaux, who was jealous of me personally, did all in his power to hamper our efforts to replace Case. I told the group how the eight Sioux tribes had agreed to go to Washington and hire a new lawyer who would properly present the claim. Near the departure date, I called John Little Cloud, the Cheyenne River Sioux's chairman of the claims committee, and he told me that no date was set for the trip to Washington. Three other tribes hedged. It turned out that I had to journey to Washington alone to file the pertinent documents on November 6, 1956, the last day before the time limit on the proceeding ran out. I found a new lawyer, and rounded up the required signatures from Sioux tribal leaders. The claim is still being pursued, and some day we may be compensated for the loss of the Black Hills. But the claim would have evaporated if it had been left to Ducheneaux, who remarked that the Sioux would lose even if they won the claims case. This was, I told

130

the assembly, an example of the regard the incumbent tribal chairman had for the welfare of the Sioux. I asked that they support Williams, who had *their* interests at heart, and would fight to obtain what was rightfully theirs.

On September 4, two days before the election, Williams and I wandered around the grounds of the annual Cheyenne River Sioux Pow-Wow and Rodeo in Eagle Butte. Williams was enthusiastically greeted by the people attending the show, and I could see the Cheyenne River police force keeping a sharp eye on us. Suddenly I heard a familiar voice booming out from a loudspeaker. It was Alfred Left Hand Bull, the man who had been impeached in 1954 for violation of his oath as president of the Rosebud Sioux, and who had been involved in the Norma Jean Le Roy accident.* He was now telling the people of Cheyenne River fantastic stories about my conduct in Indian affairs. He was bitter about his impeachment, and charged that I had lied about many people and had made complaints which were never proven. I was, he said, hurting the Sioux people.

Since Ducheneaux ran the Pow-Wow, I knew that I would not have an opportunity to answer Left Hand Bull. One Rosebud Sioux, Leo Menard, who was in the crowd, shouted that Left Hand Bull was the one who was lying. The crowd did not seem responsive to Left Hand Bull's attempt to discredit me and, by association, Williams.

Later that day we got news of a kind of tactic even we did not expect.

The tribal election committee issued a statement that denied Williams the right to vote. Furthermore, they stated that "Mr. Ramon Williams will not be seated as chairman even if he wins the election on September 6, 1966, because he is not residing on the reservation." This, of course, contradicted the committee's decision that Williams was a qualified candidate, and therefore could run in the primary. This twist was so ridiculous and incredible that we had not planned at all for such an eventuality.

Actually, the tactic of disqualifying a candidate or a voter for

* Alfred had been a passenger in the car driven by his son, Victor Left Hand Bull.

not fulfilling some residency requirement is a usual one in tribal elections. The BIA has permitted it ever since the first tribal elections were held, as provided for in the Indian Reorganization Act of 1934. But this action of the Ducheneaux administration was so brazen that even the most hardened politico would have yelped with astonishment. Williams, having been qualified to run, was now being told he did not have the right to vote, and that if he won the election he would not be seated in the position to which the people elected him. This announcement was calculated to make the Cheyenne River people think that Williams had no chance to become chairman whatsoever, and that those who were smart—wanted to keep their jobs, get their loans, or whatever—had better vote for the man who already had decided he would win: Frank Ducheneaux. The people tempted to vote for Williams, and therefore for a change in the management of the tribal affairs, would feel defeated before even touching a ballot.

Williams and I prepared a letter immediately after the announcement was made. Five hundred copies were mimeographed and distributed, and we made sure that each of the seven men who made up the election committee received a copy. The letter read: "This . . . is to officially inform you that I have reason to believe that my wife and I will not be allowed to vote on September 6, 1966, for the alleged reason that we are not qualified residents of the Cheyenne River Sioux reservation." Williams went on to assert that the election board had determined that he was a resident and could run in the primary election, and had certified him as a candidate for chairman in the general election, to be held on September 6, 1966. Williams then stated that if he were denied the vote in the general election, he intended to invoke federal statutes and go to court to prove that a conspiracy to deprive him of his rights had been allowed within the tribal administration.

September 6, 1966, the day of the general election on the Cheyenne River Sioux reservation, was clear and warm, without an ominous cloud in the sky. Ramon, his wife Ramona, his brother Maurice, Leonard Cook, and I rode in the Williams' car to the Thunder Butte polling place. We entered the log building. Ramon and Ramona Williams demanded the right to vote of the election

132

official, True Clown. True Clown stammered and seemed frightened. I stood by, taking notes on the proceeding. After agreeing that it was wrong to deny a man the right to vote, True Clown finally telephoned the election officials at the BIA agency. He said that he would try to get "them" to give him permission to allow the Williamses to vote.

True Clown returned from the telephone with a long look on his face, and told the Williamses that they could not vote. We held a quick discussion, and decided to leave the polling spot before some Ducheneaux official could trump up charges that we were making trouble. We drove to Ramon's brother's house, and we had no sooner arrived than a man came in to report that there was trouble at the Eagle Butte district polls.

Williams and his brother went over to the polls to see what was wrong. The wife of Frank Ducheneaux had refused a Vietnam veteran, Calvin Traversie, the vote. Traversie had been allowed to vote in the Primary Election, just as Williams had. Traversie got angry when told he could not vote, and a fight almost broke out as his friends joined him in his protest to the Eagle Butte district election officials. William Shaving, the election superintendent, upheld the decision to deny Traversie his right to vote, again using the "residency" requirement as the justification. Tribal police were called, and they dispersed the angry crowd that now thronged the polls.

Throughout that evening people came to Ramon Williams and told him of being deprived of their votes. As the list increased, we discussed possible legal action, and an appeal that would be filed according to the regulations of the Secretary of the Interior. Williams asked me about my attorney, John Goodrich, and decided that Goodrich was the man he would consult if legal counsel became necessary.

The results were announced. Ducheneaux's tribal election committee gave Ducheneaux a fifteen-vote victory over Ramon Williams. With this announcement came a rumor that a warrant was out for my arrest. Williams and I decided to call Goodrich and ask him to come to the reservation to help us with the preparation of affidavits from those who had been turned away from the polls, and

133

from those who had witnessed violations at the polls. Williams and his friends went out to spread the word that a meeting of those Cheyenne River Sioux whose rights had been denied would be held at 8:30 P.M., and that funds would have to be raised to carry the issue to the courts and attempt to overturn the election results.

At the meeting Williams gave the crowd a rundown of the pertinent events of the day. He urged that contributions be made, so he could continue to battle Ducheneaux and his cronies. Many present made substantial contributions and promised to help Williams in every way possible. It appeared that, for the first time in years, Ducheneaux had a fight on his hands.

Goodrich arrived in Eagle Butte that evening, and I briefed him on the election. The next morning we began the task of assembling and recording the facts that would prove the election fraudulent. People began coming to the house to swear affidavits stating the circumstances of the violation of their right to vote, and that they had intended to vote for R.L. Williams. The Williamses prepared individual affidavits, providing information that supported the fact of their residency on the reservation. Witnesses also made statements to be notarized, describing their observations of the conduct of election officials in rejecting voters who believed themselves to be qualified. Of course, all of the voters denied the ballot had intended to vote for Ramon Williams.

Person after person filed into the house to make his statement. Sandra E. Long Brake swore that she had been assaulted at the polls by the stepdaughter of Frank Ducheneaux, Mona Raye Marshall, as a tribal policeman, Charles Ducheneaux, watched. Arbana Thompson, an election clerk at Eagle Butte, reported in an affidavit that the wife of Frank Ducheneaux, Catherine Carter Marshall Ducheneaux, had been at the polls from 8 A.M. to 5 P.M., and had attempted to influence her decisions as to the qualifications of the voters. When Mrs. Thompson objected to the lack of qualifications of certain voters—who were supporters of Ducheneaux—Mrs. Ducheneaux directed William Shaving, the election superintendent, to allow those people to vote, which he did. Walter Woods, a retired Army veteran, told, under oath, how he had been informed that his election residence affidavit had been destroyed by Sidney

134

Keith, a member of the election board, thus nullifying the vote he had just cast for Ramon Williams. And so the day went, with complaint after complaint being duly recorded in the form of an affidavit and notarized.

Having your right to vote arbitrarily rescinded is a fundamental violation of the democratic process, and democracy had been badly battered on that September 6. Can you imagine the reactions of New Yorkers or San Franciscans going to the polls and finding the *candidate's wife* passing on the eligibility of voters? Can you imagine your reaction if you were told you were not a resident of your state because you had been overseas fighting for your country for two years and therefore would not be allowed to vote? The stories sworn to that day were sad indeed, sad for the Indian, but sad, too, for America, and for the ideal the white men so industriously have tried to instill in the Indian. After years of Frank Ducheneaux and his machine, and after a century of the BIA, it was amazing that any Indian like Ramon Williams, willing to fight against corruption rather than to profit from it, existed.

As we worked to collect statements from those who had observed violations, another complaint cropped up again and again. It was, in comparison to the flagrant violations, almost laughable, but the facts behind this tactic had made a good many people justifiably angry. The ballots had had Ducheneaux's name in larger print than Williams'. Just before election day, Ducheneaux had announced that he had just signed six hundred checks for Poverty Program employees. We knew that the printing of the ballots was done by people on the Office of Economic Opportunity payroll. This kind of abuse of programs which were supposed to be non-political and to help all Indians seemed to frustrate and anger people more than the unfortunately familiar self-serving, avaricious actions of politicians and officials. Perhaps the Indian people were getting the message: that there were no limits to misuse of power by the top dogs in the tribe; and the member of the reservation began to see himself as he truly is, a victim at the mercy of a callous and almost indestructible combine of white (BIA) and red ("elected" officials) men.

After filing the documents necessary to institute a recount proceeding, and receiving a date—September 30—for the recount, Williams wrote the following letter to the Bureau of Indian Affairs Aberdeen area director, Martin N. B. Holm:

> In. accordance with the Constitution and Laws of the U.S., [and the] rules and regulations of the majority of the voters of the Cheyenne River Sioux Tribe, [I] officially request that the Bureau of Indian Affairs intervene in the recount of the election returns that is to be held on September 30, 1966.
>
> I am also requesting that you contact the Commissioner and through him select several staff members to meet with our people at Eagle Butte, South Dakota, at 1:00 o'clock P.M., MST, September 29, 1966, so that we can present our evidence to prove election fraud.
>
> I am urgently requesting that you intervene, conduct, and supervise the entire recount of the election results held on September 6, 1966, because of election fraud, constitutional rights violations, misuse of federally appropriated funds, and also the use of OEO employees in a political campaign.

Williams told Holm that he would take legal action if the BIA did not fulfill its legal obligations to the members of the Cheyenne River Sioux.

John Goodrich, serving as Williams' lawyer, received a remarkable letter, dated September 9, from Raymond Heib, attorney for the Cheyenne River Sioux tribe. Heib suggested to Goodrich that the "issues" could be simplified between them, and went on to say this: "I observed from the election board that there was unanimous agreement that counting of the ballots would not result in any change of the margin of victory so perhaps we can dispense with the recount." Ducheneaux and his boys had generously allowed the recount proceeding to take place, but he obviously was not going so far as to place his election in question. The decision had been made in advance of the actual recounting of the ballots. This kind of absurdity is exactly what happened on a closely supervised Indian reservation, and the tribal attorney was brazen or stupid enough to put it in writing.

During the days that followed, more affidavits were sworn out by tribe members who had been denied the vote. Other statements

136

were gathered concerning Indians who were allowed to vote although they did not fulfill the requirements of a voter as described in the tribal constitution. Williams was advised by Goodrich to obtain proof of his residence from the county treasurer, which he did, in the form of a statement of his purchase of license plates for his car. Ramona Williams got a statement of her legal voting residence from the office of the county auditor of Ziebach County, South Dakota. Both of the Williamses had legal proof of their residency on the reservation to present at the recount hearing.

The *Rapid City Journal*, a South Dakota daily newspaper, had kept up a running report of the controversy during the period between the primary elections and the general election. They aired reports from both sides—the Ducheneaux camp and the Williams faction—and the sordid election was revealed to the public. Encouraged by the hard evidence they had gathered and the newspaper's effect on public opinion, Ramon and his supporters were beginning to feel confident about the election recount.

Then came a telegram from the BIA's Commissioner of Indian Affairs, telling Ramon Williams that the Bureau was adopting a "hands off" attitude toward the election dispute because it was an internal tribal affair. The Bureau was again showing its utter disregard for the rights and welfare of the individual Indians under its jurisdiction. No wonder the tribal officials acted with such disregard of law and justice; there was no one that they had to answer to except a "constituency" of suffering, powerless Indian people whom the tribal officials victimized. As usual, the curtain raiser had been all promises and good intentions, from Senator McGovern's assurances to the BIA's insistence on an honest election, but when the curtain was pulled down, the stage was littered with cheated, defrauded, deceived and exploited red men.

September 30, 1966, was every bit as sorry a day as Raymond Heib's absurd letter augured it to be. The election recount began with the tribal election committee denying Ramon his right to legal counsel. Goodrich and Roger Paske, an official court reporter, were escorted by armed police from the room. Councilman "Tuffy" Ducheneaux made up the laws and rules of court as the hearing went along. Williams was told that he could not have Goodrich

137

represent him because lawyers were not permitted to practice on the reservation unless they had been legal residents for one year and had paid a fee of three hundred dollars. (It was, of course, almost impossible for any tribal member to acquire legal counsel under these restrictive and expensive conditions.) As the recount proceeded, Ramon had to get up from his seat and leave the room in order to have his legal questions answered by Goodrich. The worst part of this tyrannical abuse of the law is that these qualifications for counsel had to have, of course, the approval of the local officials of the BIA, although they could have been challenged by the Secretary of the Interior. But the Secretary of the Interior was much too busy to review tribal matters, so that such laws get enacted by the Indian's guardians.

The recount was a farce. The tribal chairman, Frank Ducheneaux, knew that Ramon Williams had only a slim opportunity to institute a court action, while Ducheneaux, on his part, had the power to threaten Williams' grazing lands—so he and the tribal attorney quashed the entire recount proceeding. Regardless of the weight of the evidence Ramon produced, the tribal election committee would ridicule his assertions. After hours of indignities and abuse, the hearing came to a close. Frank Ducheneaux's election to chairmanship of the Cheyenne River Sioux tribe was approved. There had been no surprises.

The following year, in the summer of 1967, I decided to run for the office of president of the Rosebud Sioux. I knew that Cato Valandra and his cronies were firmly entrenched, and that he would battle me as ferociously and unscrupulously as Ducheneaux did in his "defeat" of Ramon Williams. Not only was a position of power at stake, but if I were to win, I would have access to the tribe's records. I estimated that approximately twenty men and women could be indicted for crimes ranging from fraud to embezzlement, and that the tribe could possibly sue to recover approximately $2 million of tribal monies that had been expended illegally. Therefore, the tribal leaders were struggling to save more than their political careers; they would be battling for their very freedom, and the prospect of a victory by anyone who intended to rid the reservation of graft and corruption understandably filled them with alarm.

In June 1967 I circulated a petition around the reservation nominating me as a candidate for the office of tribal president. People eagerly signed, even many of those who were employed within the BIA, OEO's War Against Poverty, and the tribe's offices. The campaign increased in force and fire, and Valandra soon had OEO employees (who were paid from federal funds) out on the Rosebud roads distributing handbills from house to house that described me in a variety of untrue and slanderous ways. I had marched with a group of Indians in the Peace March in New York City on April 15, 1967. This was true, but the handbills proclaimed that we had burned an American flag and our draft cards. These were lies.

A tribal election committee, hand picked by Cato Valandra, was formed. Thomas Valandra, Sr., Cato's father, was named to the board, as were Mathew War Bonnet, Justin White Hat, Francis Bordeaux, Sr., and Fred Schmidt. All of the men but Schmidt were considered to be in the pay of Cato Valandra. An outrageous fee of fifty dollars for the filing of all petitions was requested by the committee. I paid the fee and my candidacy was approved. Lawrence Antoine, a resident of Winner, also was running for president, against the incumbent, Cato Valandra, of St. Francis. Adam Bordeaux, the incumbent vice-president, was qualified as a candidate for that office, as were two other men, Iver Crow Eagle and Calvin Jones, a resident of the Soldier Creek community and the operator of a store and filling station owned by Cato Valandra. Jones was Valandra's choice as vice-president for he wished to be rid of Bordeaux, one of the rare honest and sincere officials in the tribal government.

The primary campaign was a heated one, violent on occasions. Valandra, however, stayed in the background, evidently counting on the more than seven hundred people whose jobs were dependent upon him to assure him of a primary victory. He did not want to debate the issues publicly.

The primary election was held on August 24, 1967, and went off smoothly. To everyone's amazement, I beat both Cato Valandra and Lawrence Antoine. My margin of victory was very slim; I received

139

589 votes to Valandra's 575. Antoine got 157 votes. Then the chicanery began. Ten days after the primary, the election board disqualified the entire voting population of the Horse Creek community. They had voted 18 to 2 in my favor. Now the impression was given that the primary results were reversed, and that Valandra had won. But it did not take much talk with many members of the tribe at the annual Rosebud Tribal Fair, to realize that the people *knew*, despite official announcements, that the Valandra administration had suffered a severe setback. Lies were beginning to lose their effectiveness. Valandra had lost, and all the reshuffling, manipulating, and revising of the facts could not make him appear a winner to the reservation.

The administration seemed well aware that their image as winner come-what-may was tarnished, and on the day of the Pow-Wow the tribal big shots gathered together all the employees of the Office of Economic Opportunity and told them they had better get to work in the campaign to reelect the tribal officers or their jobs would be in jeopardy.

Other people, dependent upon Valandra for employment, were assigned specific tasks that would assist the Valandra crowd in their campaign or were pressured into signing letters that made libelous statements against myself and other candidates. Tempers were rapidly reaching the boiling point, and fights between my supporters and the Valandra faction were on the verge of breaking out a number of times. Those who supported me by signing my petition or by displaying posters supporting my election were systematically harassed, not only by the tribal leaders but by BIA employees and officials. When I tried to buy space to advertise my candidacy in the Rosebud Sioux *Herald*, a tribally owned newspaper, I was told by the editor, Frank LaPointe, that he had been instructed by Cato Valandra not to permit any political advertising in the paper. About the only opportunity left for me to reach the people, other than personally, was to publish and distribute a report stating very plainly what they could expect when and if I were elected. My advantage, and I counted it a great one, was a reputation for honesty and the example of the job I had done before as tribal president. But I was continually told by hundreds of different people that the election would be rigged. I did not know how; therefore I could only hope for the best.

Unknown to me, on the day before the election, all community election committees were specially instructed on voting procedures. Attention was focused on the so-called challenged vote. Any election official could challenge a voter, place his ballot in a sealed envelope, after marking it with the name of the voter and the name of the election official, and put the vote aside.

October 26, 1967, was election day. I guessed—in fact, I knew—that I could beat Cato Valandra by at least 250 votes. I had counted just about every vote on the reservation in advance, and although there was a possibility that a good number of voters had not made their minds up yet, it was not a probability. It seemed to me highly unlikely that I would lose.

But "lose" I did. Early in the morning of the day of the election I received an urgent telephone call from an old schoolmate, Stella Quinn. She told me of the challenged vote system that was being utilized with a vengeance. I immediately drove to Winner, where the call had come from. A large number of angry Rosebud Sioux rushed up to me and told me how they had been denied their voting rights. Some had been allowed to cast ballots, only to have them challenged and stacked on the election official's table; others had been plainly denied the vote. When the report of irregularities completely unfolded, I could not believe it. It was even more astonishing, more absurd, than the scandal at the Cheyenne River Sioux reservation. The community election officials had been instructed not to allow *any* person the right to vote if he resided in Winner, Colome, Dallas, Durke, Gregory, Herrick, and St. Charles, all townsites on the reservation in Tripp and Gregory counties. Needless to say, all of these towns favored my election. Altogether at least four hundred people were denied their voting rights, and in that number was the voting population of six towns. I beat Valandra in fourteen other communities, but somehow the tally came out in his favor.

We had lost—not in the conventional, democratic way, at the

polls, but at the hands of men who would not shrink from the grossest abuse of power, through the manipulation of the polls. We had been tricked and were without legal remedies.

For days we waited for the tribal election committee to announce the official count, while they met behind closed doors, refusing to allow anyone into the room. Many of the community election officials swore that officials of the BIA were present, and were counting the ballots too. Even if this were true, it wasn't much consolation, for I didn't imagine that the local BIA people would be looking out for my interests. Harold Schunk, the BIA superintendent, had good reason to work for my defeat, since, as I have already described, I had instituted action that I hoped would lead to an indictment in the ongoing Blue Horse land swindle.

As the tribal election committee deliberated and counted, I, as Ramon Williams had done, began collecting affidavits from people in the towns mentioned before who were denied their right to vote. A petition requesting the Supreme Court of the United States and the President of the United States to protect our voting rights was circulated and 118 signatures were obtained. I filed a protest with tribal officials and demanded a hearing; they ignored my request completely. A number of people were angry enough to take matters into their own hands. I decided to appeal directly to a higher authority in the department of the interior.

On November 13, Moses Big Crow, Henry Crow Dog, my son Cleveland, and I met in Washington with Harry R. Anderson, Assistant Secretary of the Interior. We presented our evidence that the election had been rigged. He advised us to prepare a written "Notice of Appeal" and send it to him for formal consideration. We left Washington and soon mailed Anderson a four-page document asking the Secretary of the Interior not to recognize the results of the recent election. We listed all of the abuses committed by the ruling officials, in juxtaposition with pertinent passages from our tribal constitution, which defined the violations. The abuses were many—the denial of the vote to the qualified residents of the six towns was the cardinal abuse, but there was no shortage of others. Voting hours had changed; over two hundred voters were not allowed to cast their ballots secretly; my official poll watcher

142

was not allowed to enter the room where the tribal election board was tallying the election results the evening of the election; the same board refused to show me any of the election results, registration lists, voters' lists, or any of the "challenged" votes, all of which were violations of the regulations governing election procedures. We also listed a number of other violations: OEO and BIA personnel and members of the tribal election board openly participating in the election campaign, the introduction into the campaign of racial slander by Valandra (he tried to scare the reservation by saying that I would turn the reservation over to blacks), and several other instances of illegal procedures and rule violations. We might have saved our travel expenses and the time devoted to the document, for we were duly notified that the department of the interior held that the elections were legal and that the elected officials would be recognized by the BIA.

The Ducheneaux and the Valandras, blessed by lack of scruples, and the only power that could curtail their corrupt regimes, the BIA, continued to bleed the Indian and to fill their own pockets, and the pockets of their cohorts and flunkies, with the gold paid for by the Indian's blood—his land, his job, his heritage.

9
New Faces,
New Programs;
Old Problems

As the 1970s approached and arrived, things changed on the Rosebud reservation. But, as the saying goes, the more things change, the more they stay the same. Assistance projects, political upheavals, good intentions, all spun like cotton candy out of almost nothing, and dissolved rapidly into the same nothingness that the Indian has experienced for decades at the hands of his tribal government, the federal government, and the BIA.

Until the last few years, Indian tribes had been excluded from public housing assistance. Housing needs among Indians were and are acute. Great numbers of Indian families live in tarpaper shacks, tents, auto bodies, rude log huts. In 1966 federal people had made promises to the tribe that included an ambitious housing program. The tribal officials kept reminding the federal officials of their promises, and in 1967 a grand housing project for the Rosebud Sioux was begun. Plans for building 375 "Transitional Homes" on Rosebud were approved and funded with $1,700,000. Federal funds and bonds issued by the Rosebud tribe amounting to $3 million were to finance the building of the "Sioux 400" homes.* The program sounded fine, and the incumbent Valandra administration made enormous political capital from the assertion that "they" were going to supply almost four hundred new homes to the reservation in 1968.

By the end of 1969 the program was a complete failure—except to those who made criminal profits from the construction of the homes. Today there are 375 cheap, defective houses made of ⅜-inch plywood on the reservation. Ceilings are caving in, roofs leak,

---

* The "Transitional Houses" were a gift to the Rosebud Sioux, while the "Sioux 400 Homes" were financed by the sale of bonds, with some federally appropriated funds to cover administrative cost.

walls are crooked, and floor joists show through the tiles. Over three hundred of the houses do not have back or front steps. Over forty of the houses are uncompleted; they have no toilets, no plumbing or bath tubs, no cupboards or cabinets or sinks. The people who live in those "Transitional Homes" and the "Sioux 400 Homes" have complained without success to the federal government. Meanwhile, their "homes" fall down around their heads.

The housing boondoggle began with hiring practices. The tribal officers used the employment opportunities of the program to reward their faithful followers and to punish any of the tribe who fought against the corrupt regime.

The assignment of the houses was just as discriminatory. Applicants were disqualified because they were too old, too rich, or single. But applicants who were older than those turned away, who made good incomes (in some cases, employees of the federal government), and who were single but who supported the administration, were accepted. The purpose of the program, according to the government, was to house the "poorest of the poor."

The biggest swindle was cost. With federal funds guaranteeing payment for whatever jerrybuilt shack was produced, the construction people, the inspectors and overseers, and the officials who handed out contracts struck it rich. The last reported construction cost per home was $8,170—and any contractor in the country would be deliriously happy if he were offered a contract to build those homes for that much money. I wrote to Secretary of Housing and Urban Development George Romney early in 1969, reporting the discriminatory hiring situation and asking about the cost of the houses that were being built. On February 24, 1969, he answered: "Regarding your question on the cost of these homes, a study dated August 30, 1968, by Battelle Memorial Institute, concluded that the construction costs (labor and materials) were $3,400 per housing unit with additional costs of $3,170 from sources other than HUD for utilities, transportation, miscellaneous overhead and water and sanitary facilities." Romney admitted that the government, at that time, was assuming a cost of $6,570 per house. The University of South Dakota's Bulletin Number Ninety-Nine, Spring 1969, notes on page 98, "The occupants pay $5.00 per month for 5 years to the tribe. Total cost of construction is approximately $5,500." But a publication issued in September 1968 based on the final report on the Rosebud Transitional Housing Program by Father Richard G. Pates, S.J., administrator, states that the grand total cost on a completed home was $2,327. It is obvious the government doesn't know what is going on, and a good many people got rich from the Rosebud matchbox house program. The quality of construction and the outrageous costs provoked the Rosebud OEO Legal Aid Director, Bill Jenklow, to announce in several public reservation community meetings that his office was going to sue the Rosebud Housing Authority and the contractor, Park Daley, of the Daley Redwood Homes, Sioux City, Iowa. The suit was never filed.

In August 1969 the Cato Valandra administration was finally ousted. An Episcopalian minister, Reverend Webster Two Hawk, and I ran against Valandra, and both Two Hawk and I won the primary, thus eliminating Valandra from the general election. (Valandra had buffaloed outsiders into thinking he was a sterling example of an Indian leader, and he had even been appointed to presidential committees by both President Johnson and President Nixon; but evidently his people thought somewhat less of him.) I lost the general election to Two Hawk, and although the minister had loose ties with Valandra—he had been associate director of the OEO under the charge of Valandra—we rejoiced that a man who was strangling the tribe to death was out of office.

On December 1, 1969, Two Hawk took office and announced that a full report on the tribe's affairs would be made shortly.

On January 5, 1970, the Rosebud Sioux *Herald* offered the following headline: "Two Hawk Report Shows Tribe Broke, Employees Laid Off." The February 2 issue of *The New York Times* reported the findings of the newly elected president, Webster Two Hawk. In sum, Two Hawk found the following anomalies on the Rosebud reservation: the loss of 477 cattle, 52 horses, and a quantity of machinery; a $26,000 operating loss at the tribal ranch since 1964; debts of $104,000 including a $27,000 overdraft on Cato Valandra's checking account; the loss of several tribal businesses,

147

including Rosebud Electronics, Inc., and some $200,000 in letters of credit and guarantees to merchants.

Finally a Rosebud Sioux tribal officer was confirming, and the newspapers were reporting, the substance of hundreds of letters I had written to Attorney General Ramsey Clark, FBI Director J. Edgar Hoover, Secretary of the Interior Stewart Udall, and President Johnson. These top federal authorities had refused to prosecute the criminals. Indeed, at the very moment the scandal broke, Valandra was in Washington discussing Indian problems at the invitation of federal officials. Although the authorities took no action, now at least, the problems were being publicly exposed.

Unfortunately, President Two Hawk seemed prey to the frustration and hopelessness that others of our tribe had felt when attempting to obtain justice, for in an interview on January 29, 1970, with the editors of the Todd County *Tribune*, he compromised the strong stand he had taken originally. The headlines now read: "Two Hawk Says Tribe Overextended, Not Broke." Two Hawk's constituents, at that moment, sensed weakness in their president. Rumors began circulating about him, and about the supposed domestic reasons for what seemed to be indecisiveness and lack of authority.

The people of the reservation began to organize a petition calling for the minister's resignation because of his apparent inability to say "yes" or "no" to those he encountered in the course of the day's business. But the incident that was uppermost in the tribespeople's minds was the strange appropriation of a tribal firm, Rosebud Electronics, by Cato Valandra. Rosebud Electronics manufactures cables for IBM computers, and is one of the most profitable industries on the reservation. Upon leaving office, Cato Valandra incorporated this tribal enterprise as his own firm, and challenged the Two Hawk administration for its ownership. It is hard to imagine the theft of a factory, employees, and all the materials belonging to the operation, but with the United States government looking blankly on, it happened. The BIA says, "That's the Indians' own affair," but then it turns around and tells a man who wants to use land to which he is entitled, "You must own some livestock before we can allow you to use your own land."

148

This combination of a policy of outrageous interference in matters that any sensible person would consider private, and a hands-off attitude with regard to matters that represent millions of dollars and the welfare of the tribe is what galls Indians about the BIA. The agency is charged with the responsibility of "full guardianship" of Indian tribes, but it exercises that responsibility in an unrealistic and capricious manner. The Rosebud superintendent, Howard Enveau, was quoted as saying, "The Bureau serves as technical advisor as needed or wanted. . . . We are relegated to the sidelines." As the preceding chapters of this book show, this statement is composed of the same stuff we use to prepare our fields in the spring.

The war goes on. The Indians are still very much on the losing side, but they fight. A suit brought in 1968 by Frank King, Jr., Iver Crow Eagle, John Fire, and me, demanding that the President of the United States, then Lyndon Johnson, the Secretary of the Interior, then Stewart Udall, the commissioner of Indian Affairs, Robert Bennett, and the director of the Office of Economic Opportunity, Sargent Schriver, fulfill their obligations toward the Sioux Indians in accordance with the laws and treaties of the United States, is still pending. It reviews all of the important abuses and crimes described in this book, and some of those reported by Two Hawk in his statement on the status of the tribe's financial affairs. What the outcome will be, I do not know. But more and more people are becoming aware of the repression and exploitation of the Indian by the BIA, by the United States government, by white industrial and farming interests, and by those Indians who have shown us that the path to assimilation leads straight to corruption. The sound of the bugle still echoes in our ears but perhaps with the help of public opinion, strong leaders, and interested Americans, the Indian will rally and not only save himself from disaster, but also give all Americans an awareness of a beautiful and wise element of this country's heritage which has been sadly ignored.

10
Conclusion:
A Plan for the 70s

The Rosebud Sioux's long and painful fight against corruption, exploitation, and oppression stops here. But the fight does not. There will be more chapters in the story of the Rosebud reservation; perhaps the last will be a happy and victorious conclusion. This book could have been written of any of a number of Indian tribes, with different names and in different states, for each tribe has experienced what I described. What the outcome will be of all the Indian tribes' battles to save their land, themselves, and their heritage, I cannot predict with certainty. I do know that Indians now are fighting more fiercely for their autonomy and their integrity than at any time since Crazy Horse and Sitting Bull took up arms. Genuine and effective Indian leaders have appeared—the late Clyde Warrior; Mel Thom, chairman of the Piutes of Nevada; Tillie Walker, director of the United Scholarship Fund; Gloria Emerson, a fiery Navaho girl; to name a few. Forceful programs for reform, supported by all the tribes, and recognized by whites who place justice above profit, may write the chapter, sorely needed, but missing from this book.

There are two sensitive questions, quandaries really, that recur again and again when the Indian asks for protection against the "thieves" who surround him.

The first is the bizarre situation that excludes "Indians not taxed" from the remedies offered by the Constitution of the United States. Prevented from seeking the traditional legal recourse against civil and criminal acts that other Americans have, the Indian must turn to the Bureau of Indian Affairs, which, as in the cases presented in this book, tells the victim that "it is the affair of the tribe; we can't interfere." But at the same time the Indian is a citizen of the United States; he pays every tax that every other American pays, with the exception of taxes on the land that he was allotted under the Allotment Act of 1887. But even this is no special exemption, because the land that was left over from the allotments was opened to homesteaders. Those millions of acres of land, that belonged to the Indian by treaty and that are his no longer, would seem to be adequate tax for his "allotment." Thus, the Indian does have the responsibilities of other American citizens; perhaps the most striking, for it is expressly forbidden by treaty, is the obligation to bear arms for the United States. Yet Indians are not protected by the Bill of Rights. When the Indian Reorganization Act gave the tribes the right to form their own governments and to create their own constitutions, it omitted provisions for any of the legal remedies either within or without the tribe that other Americans enjoy. So reservation Indians are whipsawed between their status of a "dependent nation" within the United States, subject to the "guardianship" of the BIA, and their exclusion from the rights held by others subject to the laws of the nation. They must answer to the federal government in one guise or another for almost everything they do, down to trivial expenditures of their own money, but the federal government does not answer to Indians who protest extortion, embezzlement, election rigging, land fraud, and assorted crimes against person and property.

The second dilemma in which the Indian is trapped is the choice between "termination" and domination by the BIA. The Indians want to live as Indians, not as ersatz whites. They believe that their culture is rich and viable, and that they have many ideas that white Americans would find valuable to learn. A culture that conceives of land as both sacred and useful, but not as something at the disposal of an individual—as a resource of the nation, not of men or corporations—obviously has something to tell a people that is rapidly polluting their country out of existence. A culture that did not have or need jails, and that in conflicts between tribes made it a greater victory to slap the face of your foe than to kill him, might have something to say to a nation that has spent billions of dollars developing hydrogen bombs, napalm, and virulent germs to impress those who defy their wishes. Indians defend the BIA, because the alternative is the abandonment of the reservations by the

152

federal government and the abrogation of the treaties that ensured Indians land and services in return for Indian concessions. Termination would disperse the Indian to the cities, to be assimilated out of his culture; if he remained in his communities, he would be prey to local predatory interests. Each possibility smells of Wounded Knee.

This double bind is an everyday fact of life for the Indian tribes. How can they escape it, without destroying their Indian culture? How can they accept it and at the same time be an independent, responsible people? Indians want to conduct their own political and social affairs, to enjoy the fruits of their labor and their land, which was theirs before the Leif Ericsons and Christopher Columbuses ever blundered onto American shores. At the same time they want to contribute to the larger society that surrounds them. I would suggest that the following specific measures would support the reasonable goals of the American Indian, and help to realize them in this decade.

Initially, in the interests of justice, I would urge a congressional investigation into the entire field of Indian affairs. Such an investigation not only would reveal the abuses of the BIA, uncover scandals that would make Teapot Dome seem petit larceny in comparison, and afford satisfaction to the hitherto helpless Indian victims, but also would mobilize public opinion in favor of overdue reforms.

Next, I would recommend that the Bureau of Indian Affairs be abolished, and in its place be established a Federal Indian Commission, directly responsible to the President. It would resemble bodies like the Federal Power Commission and the Securities Exchange Commission, and its prime responsibility would be to protect the Indians' trust lands. It would be a watchdog agency.

Then I would suggest that Congress enact what might be called "The Fair Indian Act," which would include the following provisions:

First, all elected tribal officials shall be subject to the existing laws that apply to elected federal and state officials. These would include, for example, conflict of interest laws, and

153

statutes under which one could enter federal court to defend the right to run for office and right to vote laws.

Secondly, elected tribal officials shall be held accountable for any federal or tribal funds appropriated, loaned, or borrowed, and records of such transactions shall be available to the public.

Thirdly, all Indians shall have the right to seek redress beyond the tribal courts—that is, in the federal court system, right up to the Supreme Court. (Mrs. Blue Horse and Norma Jean Le Roy's children, among countless cases, would then have the opportunity to balance the wrongs done them, instead of suffering helplessly, as they did.)

Fourthly, the Indian people shall have the means to impeach any elected tribal official who violates the laws. Now only the tribal council can recall an elected official. (Since twenty-one councilmen sat idly or fearfully by while the Valandra administration illegally indebted the tribe for more than $700,-000 and spent more than $2 million of federally appropriated funds in defiance of the tribal laws and the OEO regulations, the need for this reform is especially pressing.)

Finally, federal activities having to do with the health, education, and welfare of Indians shall be assumed by the Department of Health, Education, and Welfare, where they belong.

If these measures became reality, the $2 billion expended over the past ten years for the Bureau of Indian Affairs would be drastically reduced. The Indian tribes would assume responsibility of their own affairs, and the Federal Indian Commission, instead of bureaucratically spawning costs and employees (over 22,000) like the "benevolently" despotic BIA, would have a specific, limited job to do, and the funds alloted to it would be concomitantly reduced in proportion to its specific needs.

I would ask interested American citizens to write their congressmen in support of such a program. This would be infinitely more helpful than contributing to bogus Indian organizations and clothing drives and other fripperies designed to generate a lot of self-congratulation but small assistance to the Indian.

What the Indian wants is not so complicated, nor is it so different from what other Americans want. He wants to be himself, to protect his family and his heritage from harm, to make a living of his own choosing, and to select the men who will govern the intimate aspects of his daily life. Until now, he has been prevented from doing the least, the most basic, of these fundamental activities. He fought on the battlefield and lost. He is still fighting today for the same things—his homeland, his life as an Indian—but now without weapons. Just as in the movies, he is losing again. He asks for weapons—not guns or bombs or tanks—but simply the means to make justice prevail. Is this America? If it is, then show us Indians that the truth of Equality and Justice is fact, not just cheap talk.

卌卌 *Appendix* 卌卌

[COMMITTEE PRINT]

JULY 24, 1963

: (WITH AMENDMENTS RECOMMENDED AT APRIL HEARING)

88TH CONGRESS
1ST SESSION

S. 1049

IN THE SENATE OF THE UNITED STATES

MARCH 8, 1963

Mr. CHURCH introduced the following bill; which was read twice and referred to the Committee on Interior and Insular Affairs

[Omit the part struck through and insert the part printed in italic]

A BILL

Relating to the Indian heirship land problem.

1 *Be it enacted by the Senate and House of Representa-*

2 *tives of the United States of America in Congress assembled,*

3 That (a) the owners of not less than a 50 per centum

4 interest in any land, where ten or fewer persons own un-

5 divided interests, or the owners of not less than a 25 per

6 centum interest in any land where eleven or more persons

7 own undivided interests, where all of the undivided interests

8 are in a trust or restricted status, may request the Secretary

9 of the Interior (hereinafter referred to as the "Secretary"),

10 and the Secretary is hereby authorized to partition the land

1 in kind, or to partition part of the land in kind and sell the

2 remainder, or to sell the land if partition is not practicable :

3 ~~and a sale would be in the best interests of the Indian owners.~~

4 ~~owners.~~ *Provided, That no partition or sale shall be author-*

5 *ized unless in the best interests of the Indian owners and not*

6 *detrimental to the Indian tribe.*

7 (b) When any of the undivided interests in a tract of

8 land is in an unrestricted status, the owners of not less than

9 a 50 per centum interest in the remaining undivided trust or

10 restricted interests, where ten or fewer persons own such

11 undivided interests, or the owners of not less than a 25

12 per centum interest in the remaining undivided trust or

13 restricted interests, where eleven or more own such undivided

14 interests, may request the Secretary, and the Secretary is

15 hereby authorized, ~~to sell all trust or restricted interests if~~

16 ~~a sale would be in the best interests of the Indian owners.~~

17 ~~The Secretary may also partition the land in kind, partition~~

18 ~~part of the land in kind and sell the remainder, or sell all~~

19 ~~interests if authorized to partition or sell the unrestricted~~

20 ~~interests by a power of attorney from the owner of the~~

21 ~~unrestricted interests.~~ *where he is empowered by a power of*

22 *attorney to partition or sell all unrestricted interests, to parti-*

23 *tion the land in kind, partition part of the land in kind and*

24 *sell the remainder, or to sell the land if partition is not*

1 *practicable and a sale would be in--the best interests of the*

2 *Indian owners and not detrimental to the Indian tribe.*

3   SEC. 2. *(a)* Whenever the Secretary, after receiving

4 a request to partition or sell any tract of land under sub-

5 section (b) of section 1 of this Act, is unable after due

6 effort to obtain the approval of *any owner of* an unrestricted

7 interest in such tract, he shall, upon application of the

8 persons making the foregoing request, consent to judicial

9 partition or sale of such tract if in his judgment such action

10 is in the best interests of the Indian ~~owners.~~ *owners and not*

11 *detrimental to the Indian tribe.* Where such consent is

12 granted, jurisdiction ~~over the land~~ is hereby conferred ~~on~~

13 ~~any State court of competent jurisdiction~~ *upon the United*

14 *States district court for the district in which the land, or*

15 *any part thereof, is located* to hear and determine the par-

16 tition or sale proceedings and to render judgment for partition

17 in kind or judicial sale in accordance with the law of the

18 State wherein the lands are situated. The United States shall

19 be an indispensable party to any such proceeding ~~with the~~

20 ~~right of removal of the cause to the United States district~~

21 ~~court for the district in which the land is located, following~~

22 ~~the procedure in title 28, United States Code, section 1446.~~

23 *and absent defendants may be served as provided in section*

24 *1655 of title 28, United States Code.* The proceeds of

1   sale of the trust ~~on~~ ^{or} restricted interests shall be paid to the

2   Secretary for distribution unless he waives this requirement

3   as to any of the owners thereof. If the land so partitioned

4   or sold is acquired by an individual Indian or an Indian

5   tribe, title thereto shall be taken in the manner prescribed

6   in subsection 5 (d) of this Act.

7   *(b) The tribe or the owners of undivided Indian interests*

8   *shall have a right to purchase the property being partitioned*

9   *or sold, or any part thereof, at its appraised value unless one*

10   *of the owners objects within a time to be fixed by the court.*

11   *In the event two or more rights of preference are exercised*

12   *for the same land, or in the event there is objection by an*

13   *owner, the court shall order the land sold at sealed bids or*

14   *at public auction with the right in the tribe or any Indian*

15   *owner who has previously exercised his right of preference*

16   *to meet the high bid: Provided, That if two or more elect*

17   *to meet the high bid there shall be a further auction between*

18   *them and the property shall be sold to the highest bidder. At*

19   *a sale held pursuant to this subsection,* ~~*no bid shall be con-*~~ all bids of less than 75

20   ~~*sidered for less than the appraised value.*~~ percentum of the appraised value of the land shall be rejected.

21   ~~Sec. 3 (a) If, with respect to any land transferred pur-~~

22   ~~suant to this Act there is in existence an exemption from~~

23   ~~taxation which constitutes a vested property right, such~~

24   ~~exemption shall continue in force and effect until it terminates~~

25   ~~by virtue of its own limitations.~~

1 ~~(b)~~ *Sec. 3.* Any trust interest in oil, gas, or other min-
2 erals that ~~is~~ *may be* reserved to an Indian owner in any sale
3 of land made pursuant to this Act ~~shall~~ *may* be reserved in
4 a trust status. No sale made under this Act shall include any
5 mineral estate that has been reserved to any Indian tribe by
6 any provision of law.

7 Sec. 4. For the purposes of this Act, the Secretary of
8 the Interior is authorized to represent any Indian owner (1)
9 who is a minor, (2) who is non compos mentis, (3) whose
10 ownership interest in a decedent's estate has not been deter-
11 mined, or (4) who cannot be located by the Secretary after
12 a reasonable and diligent search and the giving of notice
13 by publication.

14 Sec. 5. The Secretary shall give actual notice or notice
15 by publication and provide an opportunity for a hearing
16 before partitioning in kind or selling land, *or before consenting*
17 *to judicial partition or sale* pursuant to this Act. All sales of
18 lands made by the Secretary pursuant to this Act shall be in
19 accordance with the following procedure:

20 (a) Upon receipt of requests from the required
21 ownership interests, the Secretary shall notify the tribe and
22 each owner of an undivided Indian interest in the land by a
23 letter directed to his last known address that each such owner
24 and the tribe has a right to purchase the land for its appraised

1 value, unless one of the owners or his authorized representa-
2 tive objects within the time fixed by the Secretary, or for a
3 lower price if all of the owners agree, and that if more than
4 one owner or if one ~~owner~~ *or more owners* and the tribe
5 wants to purchase the land it will be sold on the basis of
6 sealed competitive bids restricted to the owners of undivided
7 interests in the land and the tribe unless one of the owners or
8 his authorized representative objects within the time fixed by
9 the Secretary.

10 (b) If any Indian owner or his authorized representa-
11 tive objects to a competitive sale restricted to the owners of
12 undivided interests and the tribe, the Secretary shall offer the
13 land for sale by sealed competitive bid with a preferential
14 right in the tribe or any Indian owner to meet the high bid,
15 unless one of the Indian owners or his authorized representa-
16 tive objects within the time fixed by the Secretary. All bids
17 ~~shall be rejected if no bid substantially equal to the appraised~~
18 ~~value is received.~~ *of less than 75 per centum of the appraised*
19 *value of the land shall be rejected.*

20 (c) If any Indian owner or his authorized representa-
21 tive objects to a sale by sealed competitive bid with a
22 preferential right to meet the high bid, *or if two or more*
23 *preference rights are asserted under subsection (b) of this*
24 *section,* the Secretary shall offer the land for sale by sealed
25 bids: *Provided,* That, after notice to all interested parties

1 including the tribe, the land shall be sold at auction im-

2 mediately after the opening of the sealed bids, and auction

3 bidding shall be limited to the Indian owners, the tribe, and

4 persons who submitted sealed bids in amounts not less than

5 75 per centum of the appraised value of the land. The

6 highest sealed bid shall be considered the opening auction

7 bid. No sale shall be made unless the price is equal to *or*

8 *higher than* the highest sealed bid ~~and substantially equal to~~

9 ~~the appraised value: And provided~~ *further*, That the term [Provided]

10 "appraised value" as used in this ~~section~~ shall mean the cur- [act]

11 rent appraised value of the land, said appraisal to be not

12 more than one year old.

13   (d) Title to any land acquired by a tribe or an indi-

14 vidual Indian pursuant to this Act ~~shall~~ *may* be taken in

15 trust unless the land is located outside the boundaries of the

16 reservation ~~or~~ *and* approved tribal consolidation area. Title

17 to any land acquired by a tribe or an individual Indian that is

18 outside the boundaries of the reservation and approved con-

19 solidation area ~~shall~~ *may* be taken in *trust if the purchaser*

20 *was the owner of trust or restricted interests in the land before*

21 *the purchase or partition, otherwise shall be taken in* the

22 name of the purchaser without any restriction on alienation,

23 control, or use.

24   SEC. 6. ~~(a)~~ In order to assist tribes that wish to pur-

25 chase land offered for sale under the provisions of this Act,

1 the Secretary is authorized to make a ~~loan to any tribe under~~

2 ~~the conditions stated below, provided the tribe does not have~~

3 ~~funds available in an amount that is adequate to make the~~

4 ~~purchase and is unable to obtain a loan from any other~~

5 ~~source.~~ ~~Such loans shall be made~~ *loans, subject to such rea-*

6 *sonable rules as he may prescribe,* from the revolving funds

7 referred to in section ~~10~~ *9* of this ~~Act.~~ *Act, and in accordance*

8 *with the following requirements:*

9   ~~(b)~~ *(1)* The amount of the loan shall not exceed the ap-

10 praised value of ~~the land~~ plus the value of any other property

11 the tribe may mortgage or pledge as security for the loan.

12   ~~(c)~~ *(2)* The tribe shall give to the United States a

13 mortgage on the land purchased by the tribe with the loan,

14 and on any other tribal property which the Secretary deems

15 necessary to adequately secure the loan.

16   ~~(d)~~ *(3)* ~~A~~ *The* loan shall be for a term of ~~not to exceed~~

17 ~~thirty~~ years, and shall bear interest at a rate, to be deter-

18 mined by the Secretary. ~~A~~ *The* loan need not require repay-

19 ment in equal installments, but it shall require repayment

20 according to a schedule that will fully amortize the loan

21 within the time specified. In the event of a default in the

22 repayment of the loan, the Secretary of the Interior shall

23 take such action as he deems necessary to protect the inter-

24 ests of the United States. If during the period of repayment

1 the tribe is awarded a money judgment against the United

2 States, and if the payment of any installment on the loan is

3 in default, the installment(s) in default shall be collected

4 from the appropriation to satisfy the judgment insofar as the

5 amount of the appropriation will cover the same.

6 ~~(e)~~ *(4)* Before a loan is made under this Act the tribe

7 shall submit for the approval of the Secretary of the Interior

8 a ~~master~~ plan for the use of all lands to be ~~purchased.~~ *pur-*

9 *chased and lands presently owned.* ~~No plan shall be con-~~

10 ~~sidered by the Secretary unless it has been first considered~~

11 ~~at a general meeting of tribal members called for that pur-~~

12 ~~pose, upon due notice to all adult members of the tribe, and~~

13 ~~approved by a majority of the adult members present and~~

14 ~~voting at that meeting.~~ *No plan shall be considered by the*

15 *Secretary unless it has been first considered and acted upon*

16 *favorably by a majority vote of the duly authorized govern-*

17 *ing body of the tribe, or in the absence of such a governing*

18 *body, at a general meeting of tribal members called for that*

19 *purpose upon due notice to all adult members of the tribe.*

20 Any tribe preparing a plan may call upon the Secretary for

21 technical assistance, and the Secretary shall render such

22 assistance as may be necessary. Such plan shall include pro-

23 visions for consolidation of holdings of the tribe, or acquisi-

24 tion of sufficient lands in conjunction with those held to per-

1 mit reasonable economic utilization of the land and repay-

2 ment of the loan. Such plan may be revised from time to

3 time with the approval of the Secretary.

4 SEC. 7. *(a)* Any tribe that adopts with the approval of

5 the Secretary a plan pursuant to subsection 6(e) *6(4)* of this

6 Act, or any other plan that does not involve a loan from the

7 United States but which provides for the consolidation, man-

8 agement, use, or disposition of tribal land, is hereby author-

9 ized, with the approval of the Secretary, notwithstanding

10 any other provision of law, *subject to the provisions of the*

11 *tribal constitution, if any,* to sell or encumber any tribal

12 land or other property in furtherance of such plan.

13 *(b) Tribal land in trust or restricted status, including*

14 *land acquired by a tribe pursuant to this Act may, with the*

15 *approval of the Secretary, be—*

16 *(1) sold in trust status to individual tribal members,*

17 *or*

18 *(2) exchanged in trust status for lands within the*

19 *reservation or approved tribal consolidation area which*

20 *are held by individual tribal members or other Indians*

21 *in trust or restricted status, for the purpose of effecting*

22 *consolidations of land or aiding individual tribal mem-*

23 *bers to acquire economic units or home sites.*

24 SEC. 8. The Secretary shall approve no plan pursuant

25 to this Act that contains any provision that will prohibit or

1 ~~delay a termination of Federal trust responsibilities with~~

2 ~~respect to the land during the term of the plan.~~

3 SEC. ~~9~~ 8. This Act shall not repeal any authority of the

4 Secretary under other law, but it shall supersede any limita-

5 tion on the authority of the Secretary that is inconsistent

6 with this Act. *This Act shall not repeal the laws heretofore*

7 *enacted with respect to the procedure for disposing of or*

8 *partitioning lands belonging to members of the Five Civilized*

9 *Tribes of Oklahoma and the Osage Tribe, and this Act*

10 *shall not apply to any interest in land which is subject to a*

11 *restriction imposed by such laws.*

12 SEC. ~~10~~ 9. (a) All funds that are now or hereafter a

13 part of the revolving fund authorized by the Act of June

14 18, 1934 (48 Stat. 986), the Act of June 26, 1936 (49

15 Stat. 1968), and the Act of April 19, 1950 (64 Stat.

16 44), as amended and supplemented, including sums received

17 in settlement of debts of livestock pursuant to the Act of

18 May 24, 1950 (64 Stat. 190), sums collected in repay-

19 ment of loans heretofore or hereafter made, shall hereafter

20 be available for loans to organizations of Indians, Eskimos,

21 and Aleuts (hereinafter referred to as Indians), having

22 a form of organization that is satisfactory to the Secretary,

23 and to individual Indians of one-quarter degree or more of

24 Indian blood who are not members of or eligible for member-

25 ship in an organization that is making loans to its members,

1 for any purpose that will promote the economic develop-
2 ment of such organizations and their members, or the indi-
3 vidual Indian borrowers.

4   (b) The appropriation authorization in section 10 of the
5 Act of June 18, 1934 (48 Stat. 986), as amended by the
6 Act of September 15, 1961 (75 Stat. 520), is hereby
7 amended by increasing it from $20,000,000 to $55,000,000.

8   SEC. ~~11.~~ *10.* The Secretary is authorized to execute such
9 patents, deeds, orders, or other instruments as may be
10 necessary or appropriate to carry out the provisions of this
11 Act.

12   SEC. ~~12.~~ *11.* The terms "owner" and "owners" as used
13 herein include, wherever applicable, any tribe, band, group,
14 community, or pueblo of Indians, Eskimos, or Aleuts, and
15 also include any federally chartered organizations of Indians,
16 Eskimos, or Aleuts.

17   SEC. ~~13.~~ *12.* (a) Sections 1 through ~~9~~ *8* of this Act
18 shall become effective one year after the date of its enact-
19 ment.

20   (b) The Secretary shall, prior to the effective date of
21 sections 1 through ~~9~~ *8* of this Act, notify by publication
22 Indian tribes and owners of undivided interests in Indian
23 trust or restricted land, of the rights of such tribe or owners
24 under this Act.

25   SEC. ~~14.~~ *13.* (a) The Secretary shall, prior to the con-

1 clusion of any probate proceeding conducted on or after the

2 effective date of sections 1 through 9 *8* of this Act, notify

3 each heir or devisee having an interest in such proceedings,

4 *by actual notice or notice by publication,* of his rights under

5 this Act.

6 (b) Beginning one year after the effective date of

7 sections 1 through 9 *8* of this Act, the Secretary shall sub-

8 mit an annual report to Congress setting forth the progress

9 made in the preceding year in carrying out the purposes

10 of this Act.

A PORTFOLIO
OF PHOTOGRAPHS

by

Richard Erdoes

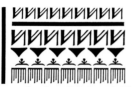 For all mankind day dawns, night falls; birth is, in time, succeeded by death. So, too, for the Indian. He, like his non-Indian fellow creatures, goes through the poet's seven ages of man. In this striking collection of photographs by Richard Erdoes, much that is perhaps peculiar to the Indian peoples is revealed, but one is forced to recognize that although the *way* differs, the essence of Indian life is that of everyman.

In Section One, a montage of faces confronts us showing Indians from infancy, through the years at life's end.

Section Two shows Indians working; sometimes performing such essential tasks as tending a store, on tribal police patrol, receiving fire-fighting assignments, herding sheep, or building a house. There are also views of Indian artisans engaged in producing useful, or merely ornamental artifacts. Some are shown firing pottery and weaving fabrics, others are stringing beads and fashioning jewelry. All, however, are producing articles bringing pleasure and a measure of esthetic fulfillment to both the creator and the user.

Section Three shows active or vicarious participation in such recreations as parading with a marching band, watching a rodeo event, playing basketball and polo, or contemplating the distracting wonders of a carnival.

Despite the impact of the white man's culture, Section Four reminds us that ancient rituals and customs have survived among the Indians. An old storyteller passes along treasured legends and memories to a youthful audience and it is likely that they, in turn, will hand down this inheritance to their children's children. Incantations are made to the spirits, traditional dances—eagle, sun, and hoop—are performed, and mystical *Yuwipi* ceremonies are enacted.

Section Five suggests the variety of dwellings to be encountered on the reservations. Some, like the summer brush shelter, log cabins, and tar paper shacks, provide but minimal protection from the elements; others (far too few) are modern homes affording comfort, convenience, and atmospheric cheeriness to the inhabitants.

Day-to-day life, as shown in Section Six, is sometimes brightened by important social occasions like a wedding, a visit with friends to talk over tribal matters or, for the children, school attendance. And many hours are consumed in that deadliest of routines—waiting: for release from a tribal jail, for attention in the offices of a bureaucracy, or to receive food supplements from an agency truck.

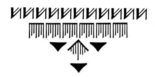

SECTION ONE

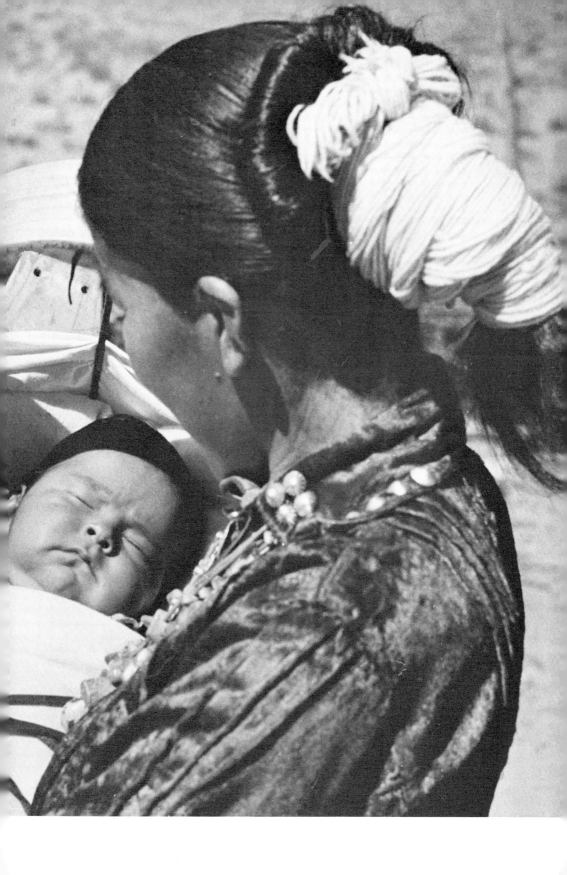

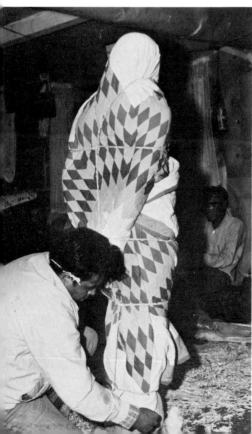